Philly Hoops
The Magic of Philadelphia Basketball

The Staff of the *Philadelphia Daily News*

Camino Books, Inc.
Philadelphia

Manufactured in the United States of America

1 2 3 4 5   05 04 03

Library of Congress Cataloging-in-Publication Data

Philly hoops : the magic of Philadelphia basketball / the staff of The Philadelphia daily news.
　　　　　p.　cm.
　　ISBN 0-940159-80-5 (trade pbk. : alk. paper)
　1. Basketball—Pennsylvania—Philadelphia. I. Philadelphia daily news (Philadelphia, Pa. : 1925)
　　GV885.73.P55 P55 2002
　　796.323'0974811—dc21

2002014142

The staff of the *Philadelphia Daily News* would like to thank the many people who loaned us Philadelphia basketball memorabilia for the cover photograph: Dave Coskey and his staff with the 76ers, Peter Capolino and the crew at Mitchell & Ness Sporting Goods, Ron Pollack, John McAdams, Cecil Mosenson, John Chaney, Michael Einbinder-Schatz, Dave Falcione, Rich Schaffer, Ted Silary, Bob Vetrone Jr., Kevin Mulligan, Don Russell, Howard Gensler and Stu Bykofsky. Special thanks also to Mike Kern and Lorenzo Biggs.

Cover and interior layout: Scribe

Photo credits for chapter openers appear on page 165.

This book is available at a special discount on bulk purchases for promotional, business, and educational use. For information write to:

Camino Books, Inc.
P.O. Box 59026
Philadelphia, PA 19102

www.caminobooks.com

Contents

About the Cover:

Authentic Julius
Erving jersey

Varsity jacket from Wilt
Chamberlain's senior year
at Overbrook

Game ball from John
Chaney's 200th victory

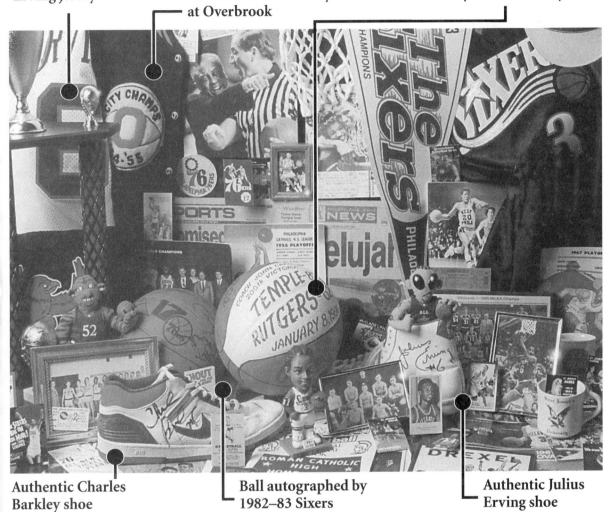

Authentic Charles
Barkley shoe

Ball autographed by
1982–83 Sixers

Authentic Julius
Erving shoe

Chapter One
The Heritage

Philly: Where Hoops Rule

RICH HOFMANN

> *"The first public exhibition was staged in the spring of 1892 but it was not until the fall of 1892 that the first teams were organized in this area and Camden gets credit for the first introduction.*
>
> *"It was at the Camden YMCA, then located on Broadway near Federal st., that members began to discuss merits of the game and decided to form a team. At that time it was not definitely decided how many men would compose a team."*
>
> — FROM THE FIRST IN A SERIES OF ARTICLES ABOUT THE EARLY HISTORY OF BASKETBALL IN PHILADELPHIA, PUBLISHED IN THE *INQUIRER* IN 1951.

It is a typical winter weekend in Philadelphia, and your basketball plate can either be full or ridiculously full. Those are the only choices.

Sixers. Drexel. La Salle. Penn. Temple. St. Joseph's. Villanova.

Small colleges. Catholic League. Public League. Rec leagues. CYO.

Girls. Boys. Men. Women. More games than you can count. More games than you can conceivably watch.

This weekend. Every weekend.

It is the only place on the continent where one Division I basketball team, the Drexel Dragons, routinely walks to a road game (at Penn). It is the only big city in America where people make a decision on whether to attend a college game based not upon what teams are playing, but the venue — and if it's at the Palestra, they go.

> ## I Remember
>
> Watching Guy Rodgers walk into my neighborhood. He would come to pick me up at my house, which was at 16th and Dauphin, and the people would start to buzz.
>
> He was a player at Northeast High at the time, but everyone knew who he was. The people would part like the Red Sea to let him by and whisper, "There he is. That's Guy Rodgers."
>
> *SONNY HILL*

With the pro team, the Sixers, as the shimmering jewel under the brightest light; with the high schools and the playgrounds and the parish gyms and the rec centers as the institutional underpinning; with all of that, nobody else has what we have. Nobody has a Big 5, for instance. Nobody has six Division I basketball teams so close together — ancient rivals in some cases, wary friends in others, all playing games that still matter, all joining together in a revival of a tradition that was sometimes dormant but never dead.

From a little first grader playing with a small ball to the Sixers, and with every stop in between, we have the opportunity to see as much basketball in person as anyone in the world, and probably more.

The wild parade that grew out of the Sixers' title in 1983.

DAILY NEWS FILE PHOTO

It is our wintertime respite. There will never, ever be anything like the old Palestra doubleheaders, when you walked into the gym on a cold January night and left about five hours later. The wind would bite you as you left. Your back would be just a little bit sore from sitting on those hard benches. And your ears — they would be ringing as you walked out the doors on the 33rd Street side and zipped up your coat, trying to trap some of the warmth inside.

The assault on your senses was unforgettable. You can never let it go. When it comes to basketball — in that way, with that everlasting memory and others — Philadelphia is about the only big city in America that really does have you from cradle to grave.

"In the fall of 1892, near the Christmas holidays, Dr. Chadwick introduced the game at the Central Y, then located at 15th and Chestnut sts.

"There was an enthusiastic crowd at Central Y and so much interest had been taken in the new game that it was decided to form a league in conjunction with West Branch Y.

"The first few weeks of this first league, 'the game was supposed to help calm down highly excited individuals and teach them to be cool, in other words to curb temper.' This it failed to do — in the league."

Philly crowd favorite Allen Iverson

GEORGE REYNOLDS / DAILY NEWS

It's played everywhere, but it's about the city. It's about the inner city, frankly. And when you look at that, the evolution makes sense.

In this city, in most big cities, basketball was a game first dominated by Jewish players and then by black players. Why? Well, as the century turned, European immigrants formed the backbone of the Northeastern inner city. Then, as the migration of Southern blacks up to Northern industries took place, the changeover occurred.

And so it happened in basketball, too. As such, the legacy of both groups is substantial.

You talk about Philadelphia basketball in the early decades of the 1900s and you talk a lot about the SPHAs, a team originally sponsored by the South Philadelphia Hebrew Association, a team organized by a 20-year-old kid named Eddie Gottlieb who would end up coaching and owning the original Philadelphia Warriors and putting his personal stamp on the NBA well into the 1970s.

The man knew basketball and the man knew Philadelphia. So Gottlieb, a power in the early NBA as the Warriors' owner, could massage the rules in a way that this city never was handicapped. For instance, he invented the idea of the territorial draft, where NBA teams had first crack at college players from their area. It was a huge advantage for the Warriors. What area had more top-level college teams than here? The answer: none. And so, Tom Gola, Paul Arizin, Guy Rodgers and more stayed home.

St. Joseph's coach Jack Ramsay

TEMPLE URBAN ARCHIVES

But here was the essence of Gotty. When it became clear that a fellow from Overbrook High School named Wilt Chamberlain would be attending college out of the area, the territorial rule was quickly changed to include high school players as well. Gottlieb's fingerprints were all over the change.

Gottlieb was still making up the NBA schedules for the league office — doing it with a pencil and paper, not a computer — when he died in 1979. Of course, everything had changed by then. Black players dominated and stars dominated — and no one epitomized the combination any better than Wilt Chamberlain, the greatest athlete ever produced by this city.

Charles Barkley high-steps off the court after a 1986 victory.

DAILY NEWS FILE PHOTO

Jerome Richardson hugs a friend after Ben Franklin wins the 1984 Public League title.

Gottlieb to Chamberlain, then. If you hadn't known who they were, standing next to each other, you never would have gotten the connection.

"In the excitement of play the players became overzealous and a game ended with a fist fight in which nearly every player joined. This caused Dr. Chadwick to issue an order that no more games would be allowed at Central Y.

"But this order did not prevent advancement of interest in the game and in 1894 there were games at Germantown Y; Temple College, Broad and Berks sts.; Hancock, Frankford ave. and Adams st.; Central High School formed its first team; Conshohocken Pioneers had a team PRRYMCA, and in South Jersey, Millville and Bridgeton began organizing, also Trenton."

As Chamberlain wrote in his book, *A View from Above*:

"I am often asked what was the best team I ever saw play. It happens to be one I was associated with. The Philadelphia 76ers of 1967–68 were without a doubt the greatest ever. Luke Jackson was the epitome of the power forward. Our guards were Hal Greer, who could shoot the lights out; Wali Jones, who played defense like a madman; and Larry Costello, an awesome outside shooter. Chet Walker was the ultimate one on one player. Billy Cunningham was the greatest sixth man in the game and was a coach on the floor. Alex Hannum, our real coach, rounded out this outstanding group."

Oh, and there was Wilt.

Oh, and five years after 1967, there also was the worst team in NBA history. They were also 76ers.

At some levels, winning has never been what the Philadelphia basketball experience has been about. That has never been the attraction. There have been a couple of championship teams at the NBA level, most recently in 1983. Villanova won the NCAA championship in 1985, and La Salle and Temple both earned their pieces of national-level hardware. But that's not really what it's ever been about.

Youngsters improvise for a hoop on the 8500 block of Williams Avenue.

Villanova coach Rollie Massimino

ALLSPORT

The competition has always been the thing, the notion of neighbor against neighbor, the idea that a college player could lose a game in February and have to hear about it for an entire summer on the various courts of this city. The competition has always been the thing. The underdog has always been the thing.

Penn beat North Carolina in the second round of the 1979 NCAA Tournament — in Raleigh, North Carolina. Steve Donches, a deep sub for St. Joe's, hit the game-winner in the 1966 Holy War against Villanova — a shot so improbable that the photographs of the moment barely catch Donches in the frame.

In 1968, the North Catholic junior varsity — playing because the entire varsity team had been suspended — still managed to win a Catholic League playoff game over Bishop McDevitt. In 2001, a Sixers team held together by adhesive tape and an unshakable belief captured the heart of a city by making it to the NBA Finals.

It has been about the competition. And this might be the only city in the world where you could put a high school JV team and the Sixers in the same paragraph and get away with it.

" . . . eight of the best teams in the city held a private meeting and the first Philadelphia League was formed with Columbia Field Club, East Falls, Jasper, St. John's, Greystock, St. Simeon, Xavier and Covenant Guild as the participants . . .

"This league drew capacity houses although the majority of the halls were small, holding from 300 to 500."

The St. Joe's cheering section roars encouragement.

GEORGE REYNOLDS / DAILY NEWS

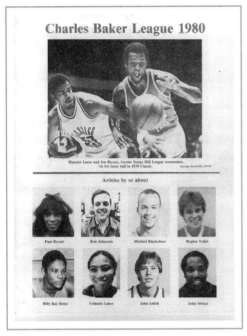

Charles Baker League 1980

Maurice Lucas and Joe Bryant, former Sonny Hill League teammates, vie for loose ball in 1979 Classic. *George Reynolds photo*

Articles by or about

Pam Bryant | Bob Johnston | Michael Blackshear | Regina Tobin

Billy Ray Bates | Yolanda Laney | John Smith | John Stokes

You can draw these lines all day: Gottlieb to Chamberlain, Chamberlain to Billy Cunningham, Cunningham to Julius Erving, Erving to Moses Malone, Malone to Charles Barkley, Barkley to Pat Croce, Croce to Allen Iverson, Iverson to who-knows-where?

That's the other thing about Philadelphia basketball: longevity.

There is just this unmatched institutional memory. The number of people who have been around seemingly forever is truly impressive.

Sonny Hill, the unmatched impresario.

Harvey Pollack, the statistician's statistician.

Bob McKee and that red cap, keeping the scorebook straight since the mid-'50s at the Palestra.

Bob Vetrone Sr., who helped to birth the Big 5 when he worked at the *Bulletin*.

Jack Scheuer of the *Associated Press*, who has reported on more basketball games in this town than anyone.

And that only begins to scratch the surface. The following list arrives in no particular order: Al Shrier and Andy Dougherty, Ted Silary, John McAdams and Dan Baker, John Chaney and Fran Dunphy, Speedy Morris and Bill Ellerbee, on and on and on. Some of these names mean something to people outside of Philadelphia, but most don't. And the thing is, we don't care.

Three priests make their voices heard in the Roman cheering section during a 1974 game at the Palestra against West Philadelphia.

DAILY NEWS FILE PHOTO

Because they are about Philadelphia basketball, which can be kind of an insular thing sometimes. You might have lived here a long time, but if you don't know how John Smith, the kid from St. Joe's, described the shot he made to defeat DePaul in the NCAA Tournament in 1981, you are still viewed with a bit of a wary eye.

(Smith called it a 4th-and-Shunk layup, by the way. But then, if you've read this far, you already knew that.)

But look at that list of names — and add your own personal favorites; feel free. They are about us. They have lived it, every one of them. They have lived it and breathed it and they remember it. And because of them, and so many others like them, so do we.

Basketball in Philadelphia is a pastime for some but a passion for so many others. It's about history and it's about opportunity and it's about that ridiculously long list, from the Sixers to the CYO. Cradle to grave.

> ## I Remember
>
> Obviously, I wasn't born yet, but the most memorable moment in Philadelphia basketball history has to be Wilt Chamberlain's 100-point game. As far as college basketball, St. Joseph's game-winning layup as time expired in their NCAA Tournament win over DePaul (1981) still ranks up there as a great moment. Personally, taking a UMass team into McGonigle Hall and holding Temple to its lowest-scoring night in the building.
>
> *JOHN CALIPARI*
> *Memphis coach*

"There was a battle between Central High and Roman Catholic (in 1908) and the two teams finished in a tie for first place. During the season Roman had defeated Central twice.

"The National Athletic Club at 11th and Catherine sts. was secured for the playoff and 4000 attended the game. The first half ended in a tie and so did the second half, so an extra five-minute period had to be played.

"Central High won. It was one of the greatest school games ever played."

All-time Philly crowd favorite Theresa Shank, who won three titles in the mid-1970s at Immaculata.

COURTESY OF IMMACULATA COLLEGE

Chapter Two

The Professionals

New Blossoms Continue to Open from Franchise with Deep Roots

PHIL JASNER

From the old Broadwood Hotel to the First Union Center.

From Cy Kasselman to Allen Iverson.

From Eddie Gottlieb to Larry Brown.

From the SPHAs to the Warriors to the 76ers.

From 10-cent hot dogs to Allen Iverson Celebriducks.

Those are some of the roots of pro basketball in Philadelphia. From a local game featuring the SPHAs (the South Philadelphia Hebrew Association) followed by a dance at Broad and Wood Streets to center stage at the First Union Center on a worldwide stage.

The impact has stretched from the late 1940s through today. It has ebbed and flowed. The last time it ebbed, the seemingly indefatigable Pat Croce emerged as the president of the Sixers, using Barnum & Bailey and Walt Disney precepts to breathe life and energy into what had become a dormant franchise.

From 1996–97 to now, the Sixers have set franchise attendance records that are continuing to mount. No team in any sport in the city's history captured the imagination and the fascination of the public the way the 2000–01 Sixers did, and they didn't even win the NBA championship.

But, with Brown coaching as if he were the maestro of a 12-man orchestra, they won 56 games and got to the Finals for the first time since 1982–83. With Iverson becoming the league's Most Valuable Player and Brown the Coach of the Year, they created a remarkable bond with the fans. People who loved the Sixers had team flags hanging from their front porches, attached to their cars and trucks, their mailboxes. The flags showed up in storefronts, pasted in windows and on coats and jackets.

"I said it when I became the president, that we had to have a rejuvenation of pride in the city, not just pride in the team," said Croce, who relinquished his duties in the summer of 2001. "We needed people to feel good about Philadelphia, to feel good about the team. The passion came back, and it was a passion that transcended the game.

"When the Sixers won the title in '83, only the real basketball fans knew. Now, the game is global, the interest is global. It's a whole new mindset. We had a team with such an unbridled spirit, it became the darling of the country. People who weren't even basketball fans were talking about the Sixers."

Even in the down years — the 1972–73 Sixers set a record for futility by finishing 9–73 — there was still a core group waiting eagerly for the next wave of success. Never mind that there was a time when the Sixers played home games as far away as Pittsburgh and Scranton in Pennsylvania, and Tulsa, Oklahoma, and even once in Yardley, Pennsylvania; when the Warriors played some home games in Hershey, Pennsylvania; Saratoga Springs, New York; and even once in Fallsington, Pennsylvania; when the Harlem Globetrotters were the featured attraction of doubleheaders.

"The loyalty of the fans is a barometer," said Sonny Hill, a senior adviser to the Sixers and one of the founders of the Charles Baker Summer Pro League. "To me, it's a basketball town. [The 2000–01] Sixers were as impact-

---

I Remember

I think my fondest and most vivid memories of Philadelphia would involve things that happened at St. Joe's. I would say there were two things that maybe stand out. The first year of the Big 5 when we beat Temple. Both of us went in 3–0 [in the Big 5], and they were ranked No. 1, 2 or 3 in the country all season, and we had a good team, but they were a national team . . . and we beat them in a great, great game at the Palestra. That made us Big 5 champs in that first season [1955–56]. The players on that team, Kurt Englebert and Al Juliana, both of whom have passed away, Bill Lynch, Dan Dougherty and Mike Fallon. Those were the starters. And, of course, Temple had [Hal] Lear, [Guy] Rodgers, Jay Norman, [Tink] Van Patton, [Hal] Reinfeld. That was an explosive beginning to the Big 5.

The other was a game in which we beat Bowling Green [December 26, 1962]. They had Nate Thurmond and Howard Komives. Again, we were a good but not great team, but we beat a very good team that night with two great players on it. And the way we won it [on a Jim Boyle floating jump shot at the buzzer].

JACK RAMSAY
ESPN analyst

ful as any team in town in history. When you talk about Philly, you talk about kids shooting hoops. The game has gone from generation to generation, from ethnic group to ethnic group."

The beginnings, Sid Gersh recalled, were far more modest. Gersh, a regular in the front row behind the scorer's table in the First Union Center, has held season tickets for 56 years. He started out in the third row, helped sell tickets and got upgraded to the front row. The president of the Jewish Basketball League alumni, he still proudly holds 10 tickets.

"When it started, it was like a Jewish night out," Gersh said. "Families were started at those games. I remember the SPHAs had a player named Gil Fitch, who also led the band at the dance afterward.

"Everybody who came to the game stayed for the dance. The big thing was to walk up the steps in the back and get a 10-cent hot dog. That was a big night out."

The Warriors won two championships, but the celebrations were strictly local and modest. The

Darryl Dawkins left his mark here.

DAILY NEWS FILE PHOTO

Former star player Billy Cunningham coached the Sixers to the 1982–83 title.

DAILY NEWS FILE PHOTO

Sixers won titles in 1966–67 and 1982–83. The parade down Broad Street after the '83 title was memorable, people celebrating wildly along the route.

Billy Cunningham, who played with the '67 team, coached the '83 team.

He remembers what he described as "tunnel vision" through those experiences, regretting he didn't take the time to enjoy them as they were unfolding. As the Sixers' magic captured the attention of people in 2001, he reminded friends in the organization not to make the same mistake.

"As players and coaches, all we felt was relief when we won," Cunningham said. "Watching the Sixers [in 2001], I saw how uplifting it was for people. I saw people making their schedules based around the games."

Pat Williams, now a senior vice president with the Orlando Magic, was the Sixers' general manager in 1976 when they acquired the legendary Julius Erving. Williams was still the GM when the Sixers, having failed in three appearances in the Finals in 1976–77, 1979–80 and 1981–82, finally won in '83.

"We captured the fancy of a nation, with the emotion toward Julius, the fascination with Moses Malone," Williams said. "[The 2000–01] team was a rebirth."

I Remember

One of my most vivid memories, I was a junior at La Salle High School, 1946. The war had ended, GIs were flowing back. We were playing Southern High for the city championship, and the largest crowd in the history of Pennsylvania basketball was there. We had to get the police to get us into the game. Southern had Stan Brown, who went right from high school to the pros. We had 13,000 there that day. [Remember] the many city games, the many big games at Convention Hall, [seeing] Western Kentucky, Bowling Green, Manhattan, St. John's, UCLA, all come in to play La Salle. Seeing San Francisco before the [Bill] Russell days. They were very good in 1949 and 1950. I was on that La Salle team that Paul Arizin got cut from. He was a senior, the last player cut. Even with that, we won everything that could be won, won the Catholic League, the city championship, the Eastern States Catholic Invitational in Newport, R.I. It was the biggest postseason tourney. We won all three. The weirdest part was, Paul was cut from the team and Nick McGuire didn't make the team either. He's in Villanova's Hall of Fame. Imagine if we had had those two.

JIM PHELAN
Mount St. Mary's coach, Philadelphia native

Cream of the Crop for Sixers/Warriors

1. Wilt Chamberlain

See the top 10 all-time players from the area. Any questions?

2. Julius Erving

Everyone says Larry Bird, Magic Johnson and Michael Jordan saved the NBA; I say Dr. J built the bridge, joining the Sixers in 1976–77. Everyone revels in Jordan's highlight-reel dunks; I say, go back and look at the early tapes of Doc and you'll see all that and more.

3. Moses Malone

He wasn't a Sixer long, but his impact in 1982–83 was beyond remarkable. On the first day of training camp at Franklin & Marshall College, he looked at then owner Harold Katz and said, "Don't worry, we'll win about 70." They won 65, and their first title since '66–67. He was on a mission that season like no player I've ever seen.

Moses Malone made a major impact in his short time with the Sixers.

DAILY NEWS FILE PHOTO

4. Billy Cunningham

There was a day at practice in 1982–83 when, while the players were conducting a meeting, the coach was shooting jumpers. Andrew Toney, one of the star guards, politely asked: "Coach, did you used to play?" Yes, he did. The "Kangaroo Kid" spent the first seven seasons of his career with the Sixers, the sixth man on the '66–67 title team. He spent two seasons in the ABA, then came back for two more with the Sixers. He averaged 20.8 points and 10.1 rebounds with the Sixers, blowing apart the theory that white men can't jump.

5. Paul Arizin

Won two scoring titles, one before spending two years in the military, one after returning. Played 10 seasons, was an All-Star 10 seasons.

6. Hal Greer

Played 10 of his 14 seasons with the Sixers, finished with 21,586 points. A seven-time

Wilt Chamberlain was tough for even Bill Russell to defend legally.

DAILY NEWS FILE PHOTO

Allen Iverson, wearing No. 6 in honor of Julius Erving, at the 2002 All-Star Game.

DAILY NEWS FILE PHOTO

Andrew Toney, the "Boston Strangler"

DAILY NEWS FILE PHOTO

All-Star as a Sixer with a jump shot so dependable, he even used it as his foul shot.

7. Charles Barkley

In 1986–87, at 6-4$^7/_8$, he became the shortest player in the modern era to win a rebounding title. He spent the first eight years of his career with the Sixers, was an All-Star in six of them and a first-team All-League selection in four. He did things a player his size wasn't supposed to be able to do.

8. Allen Iverson

The Official NBA Register lists him as 6 feet tall; he's barely that. But he has already won two scoring titles, was the league's Most Valuable Player in 2000–01 and is arguably the fastest man with the ball in the game today.

9. Maurice Cheeks

Played the first 11 seasons of his career with the Sixers without an ego; he just directed the team, played terrific defense, always found open teammates and shot only when absolutely necessary. He was the quarterback of the '82–83 title team.

10. Andrew Toney

Gone too soon because of recurring foot problems. Succeeded Lloyd (now World B.) Free as the "Boston Strangler." Never cared where the game was, or who the opponent might be. Averaged 15.9 points and shot 50 percent in his career; without the injuries, those numbers would undoubtedly be higher and we'd be discussing his entry into the Hall of Fame.

— *Phil Jasner*

Best of the Sixers/Warriors Coaches

1. Billy Cunningham

He was a driven man in 1982–83, so intense in his mission that he lost more than 15 pounds during the playoffs. When he became the coach after six games of '77–78, succeeding Gene Shue, he made Chuck Daly and Jack McMahon his assistants and mentors. He learned magnificently, finishing with a record of 454–196, taking the Sixers to the Finals in '80 and '82 before winning the title in '83.

2. Alex Hannum

He coached the Sixers for only two seasons, but was 130–33, leading them to the 1966–67 title. Was willing to challenge anyone, including Wilt Chamberlain. Died January 18, 2002.

3. Larry Brown

He breathed life into a dormant franchise, taking over in 1997–98. The Sixers somehow won 49 games in 1999–2000 and 56 games in 2000–01, going to the Finals for the first time since '83. Widely recognized as one of the finest teachers of the game.

4. Jack Ramsay

Succeeded Alex Hannum, and was 174–154 in four seasons; came back to haunt the Sixers, coaching the Portland Trail Blazers past them for the 1976–77 title. Somehow, he was never really appreciated for his work with the Sixers.

Larry Brown has helped the Sixers ascend to greatness.

G.W. MILLER III / DAILY NEWS

5. Eddie Gottlieb

Props to the man who made everything else possible. He owned the old Warriors, coached them, ran the business, etc. Maybe he wasn't a coach in the true sense of the word, but he led them to the 1946–47 title. He's on this list for historical significance.

— Phil Jasner

Sixers/Warriors Teams for All Seasons

1. 1966–67 Sixers
They were 68–13, with Wilt Chamberlain, Luke Jackson, Billy Cunningham, Hal Greer, Chet Walker and Wally (Wali) Jones.

2. 1982–83 Sixers
They won 65 games, with Moses Malone providing the missing ingredients. But Malone always deferred, saying it was "Doc's team." And it was.

3. 1976–77 Sixers
They were the greatest show on earth. Fans used to come early just to watch them dunk in the layup lines. "Showtime" before the Los Angeles Lakers ever thought of the term. Check them out: Julius Erving, George McGinnis, Doug Collins, Lloyd (now World B.) Free, Steve Mix, Henry Bibby, Caldwell Jones, Joe Bryant and, yes, Darryl Dawkins.

4. 1967–68 Sixers
Won 62 games with Wilt Chamberlain averaging 24.3 points, 23.8 rebounds and 8.6 assists, and shooting 59.5 percent from the floor. But they lost the Eastern finals in seven games to the dreaded Boston Celtics; the Celtics trumped the Los Angeles Lakers in six for the championship.

5. 1955–56 Warriors
Just to have a sense of history. You could make an argument for the '81–82 Sixers or the '79–80 Sixers, who both lost to the Lakers in the Finals, but these Warriors were 45–27 in an eight-team league when rivalries were intense. Paul Arizin averaged 24.2 points, Neil Johnston 22.1, and Johnston turned in 12.5 rebounds.

— *Phil Jasner*

(The preceding three lists were compiled with input from John Nash, Jack Scheuer, Jack Ramsay and Sonny Hill.)

I Remember

Two things. First time, I was a student at St. John's, and we just decided one day to drive down to the Palestra to see St. John's. They had Billy Schaeffer, St. Joe's had Mike Bantom. So we bought some student tickets and went down, and it was just unbelievable. We were used to the Garden, but walking into the Palestra there was such a different feeling. It was a great game, went down to the wire before St. Joe's won [76–65, February 21, 1973].

Then [on December 8, 2001], I got to go down to the day of the tripleheader. That was very special. There are a lot of great things about New York basketball, a lot of good rivalries . . . but nothing like you have down there. So it was those two things. My first visit and my most recent visit.

JIM O'CONNELL
Associated Press basketball writer

Season for All Ages

The best single-season individual performances by a Philadelphia player

1. A nifty 50

Wind him up and he cranked out 50 points a game, night after night. No player in NBA history — not Michael Jordan, not Kareem Abdul-Jabbar, not anyone — was a more prolific scorer than Wilt Chamberlain in 1961–62, when he averaged 50.4 points.

2. Best of the best

Wilt was the focal point of the team that was voted the best in NBA history — the 1966–67 Sixers. He averaged 24.1 points, 24.2 rebounds and 7.8 assists for that legendary powerhouse.

3. Nothing artificial about A.I.

He's a foot shorter and 120 pounds lighter than Wilt was, but Allen Iverson's luminous skills carried the overachieving Sixers to the NBA Finals in 2001. A.I. led the NBA in scoring at 31.1 points per game, but, more important, he was the league and All-Star Game MVP.

Wilt Chamberlain produced three of our top five single-season performances.

DAILY NEWS FILE PHOTO

4. Pass it down

Angry at too often being chided as a selfish player only interested in his scoring totals, Wilt decided that he would reinvent himself as a playmaker during the 1967–68 season. He averaged a league-best 8.6 assists.

5. Jump it up

Officially measured at 6-4$^7/_8$ inches, Charles Barkley sometimes seemed as wide as he was tall. But the Sixers' erstwhile "Round Mound of Rebound" bodied up in the paint well enough to lead the NBA with 14.6 rebounds per game in 1986–87.

— *Bernard Fernandez*

Pat Croce: Top Five Memories of His Sixers Presidency

1. Winning the lottery in '96
"I knew that we had a ton of luck, because now we would have Allen Iverson as the No. 1 pick."

2. Hiring Larry Brown as the coach in '97
"I told him I wanted him to create a legacy, the way Billy Cunningham did."

3. The first home game of the '99 playoffs against Orlando
"The First Union Center was so loud, I've never heard it louder since."

4. Game 7 of the 2000–01 playoff series against Toronto
"The whole season hung on one shot." You might recall that the Raptors' Vince Carter missed, and that the Sixers eventually went to the Finals.

5. Winning Game 1 of the Finals against the Lakers in Los Angeles
"We accomplished what everyone believed we couldn't."

— Phil Jasner

Pat Croce

DAILY NEWS FILE PHOTO

Pat Croce: Five Favorite Sixers to Train

(Before Croce became the team president, he was the strength and conditioning coach in the mid-1980s.)

1. Julius Erving
"He'd do everything. Any time. Anywhere."

2. Andrew Toney
"I was first hired to work with him [to rehab a fractured foot]. People seemed afraid because he was quiet. I enjoyed him."

3. Charles Barkley
"Because I had to be a psychologist, a magician and a friend to get him to do anything."

4. Jeff Ruland
"Because he was so intense, fighting to keep his career alive."

5. Lloyd (now World B.) Free
"Because I got to make him throw up, I got him to work so hard. He had never worked hard."

— Phil Jasner

Philly's Fraternity of Stars in Stripes

Every time Joe Crawford blows his whistle, he sees the late Joe Gushue in his subconscious. "When I broke into the NBA as a referee, Joe was the one who taught me, showed me things — big things, little things," Crawford said.

"Every game I work, Joe's face comes into my head, telling me something; how to handle a play, whether a play was goaltending or not, things like that.

"He must have told me a thousand things. I wrote them all down. I never thought Joe got enough credit for what he did."

Crawford is from Havertown, a breeding ground for NBA referees such as Tim Donaghy, Mike Callahan and Mark Wunderlich. The Philadelphia area has been a breeding ground for pro referees, in part because of a variety of opportunities to learn in high school, summer and college leagues and recreation centers.

"It's an area that has basketball year-round," said Eddie Rush, the league's chief of officials, a former referee who is also from the area. "You can go from Gustine Lake to A & Champlost to the Baker League to all the schools and colleges; young officials have opportunities. Years ago, the old Eastern League was running, so there was another chance to get involved. We look all over for good young officials, but there's still no place like this. We have Eddie Malloy from Philadelphia Textile [now Philadelphia

University] working in the developmental league. He has what I call a high basketball IQ, and his sense of the game is exceptional."

Darryl Dawkins played the pivot for the 1976–77 Sixers, one of the most memorable teams in franchise history.

DAILY NEWS FILE PHOTO

There are other factors that have been at work over the decades. "I think it goes back to the old days, when the best basketball was played in the area," said referee Steve Javie, who prepped at La Salle High and Temple. "The refs saw all the best players and got better just by refereeing the games. That, and the way the Philly guys are willing to pass down the craft. It really has become a unique fraternity."

Crawford remembers how he got started. "I was 19, Jake O'Donnell, a great referee from Clifton Heights, came to see me work a game," Crawford said. "Imagine you're 19, something like that happens. Young people in the area now can say, 'If Jake can make it from Clifton Heights, if Joe can make it from Havertown, maybe I have a chance.'"

Crawford recommended Wunderlich as a prospect after watching him work a summer league game.

But beyond that, Crawford likes the idea that referees — who by the nature of their profession are rarely interviewed or featured, unless they're involved in a controversial play — should be included in a history of Philadelphia basketball.

And every time he thinks about the profession, he thinks about Joe Gushue, and all the lessons handed down from generation to generation.

— Phil Jasner

An Official Who's Who

Best of the referees who are native Philadelphians

1. Joe Gushue
The mentor. "He did things in a way that didn't demean you," says Ed Rush.

2. Joe Crawford
The best of his time. Rush: "He has a tremendous feel for bringing out the best in his partners."

3. Jake O'Donnell

Always in charge. Rush: "He knew what to call, when to call it and was tremendous under pressure."

4. Earl Strom

The personality. Crawford: "He could have a beer with a coach, and throw him out of the game the next night. A great trait."

5. Ed Rush

The chief of officials. Crawford: "When you got your schedule of games, you looked to see when he would be your partner."

6. Steve Javie

"He'll end up being the best of all time," Crawford says.

7. Jack Madden

A big-game ref with mentoring skills. Rush: "He was exceptional in big games, and had mentoring skills before they were popular."

Joe Crawford: "Philly guys are willing to pass down the craft."

ALLSPORT

(This list was compiled with input from Joe Crawford and Ed Rush.)

Numero Uno

Former Warriors and 76ers publicist Harvey Pollack long has been known as the sultan of statistics. The more esoteric the category, the more likely Harvey is to compile data. "Once something starts going into my book," Pollack said, "it never comes out."

Here are five examples of Pollack's legendary numbers-crunching.

Harvey Pollack

1. Plus-minus for NBA players

Yeah, it's an official stat in the NHL, where a 7–5 game is considered a high-scoring affair. Pollack keeps track of the same numbers in the NBA, a considerably more taxing task. "One guy could be, like, a plus-483 and another a minus-685," he said. We'll take his word for it.

2. Distance of every field goal made

You want to know how many 20-footers Allen Iverson sinks compared to, say, 24-footers, Harvey's the guy. He also can differentiate between Shaquille O'Neal's dunks, layups and tap-ins.

3. Altered shots
Dikembe Mutombo swats 'em away, but Harvey can tell you to the last rejection whose shots are being misdirected.

4. Technical fouls
Sure, the Portland Trail Blazers' Rasheed Wallace collects a lot of them, but technicals were not an official NBA statistic until 1970, when Harvey and his crew made them so. "I wish I had been able to keep them when [the Boston Celtics' Red] Auerbach was coaching, because he had a mess of them," Harvey said.

5. Four-point plays
The three-point shot was instituted in the NBA in 1979. Harvey can tell you every player who ever was fouled on a made three-pointer, then hit the free throw.

— Bernard Fernandez

Acts of God, Man and Chocolate Thunder

Home Sixers games that were delayed, postponed or moved

February 5, 2001
A snowstorm causes a one-hour delay of a game against Denver. Allen Iverson arrives less than five minutes before tipoff due to poor driving conditions, but goes on to score 37 points in a 99–80 victory.

January 8, 1996
A blizzard along the Eastern seaboard forces the postponement of a game against Orlando. The Magic players are stranded in Allentown, Pennsylvania. It's a blessing for the Sixers, who are 6–24 and losers of 11 of their previous 14 games.

February 20, 1985
With 7:03 remaining in the third quarter against Golden State, Charles Barkley grabs the rim to avoid injuring himself on an off-balance dunk. He jars the backboard and basket support 6 inches out of position. The game is delayed for 22 minutes as the 2,200-pound apparatus is moved back into place.

December 5, 1979
A game against San Antonio is delayed as Darryl Dawkins shatters his second backboard in less than a month. (He had broken one in Kansas City on November 13.) Says Dawkins, "My contract will be up pretty soon and I want to prove that I can put people in the seats."

March 3 to March 31, 1968

Six regular-season games and several playoff games are played in either Convention Hall or the Palestra after part of the roof blows off the Spectrum.

November 22, 1963

A game against the Boston Celtics is postponed due to the assassination of President John F. Kennedy. The game is later played on March 3, 1964. The Celtics win, 108–94.

— *Mark Kram*

A Master Dribbler of the Language

Dave Zinkoff was the Sixers' voice from on high

Dave Zinkoff

DAILY NEWS FILE PHOTO

The first time I met Dave Zinkoff, he slipped me the Salami. Let me explain . . .

The ubiquitous public address announcer for the then Philadelphia Warriors, Temple Owls and anything else with a gym and a microphone that could benefit from a gentle man with a distinctive voice, always carried a spare salami or two in his briefcase.

"Have a salami, young man," Zinkoff would rasp in a voice trapped somewhere between ringmaster for P. T. Barnum and ringside professional wrestling announcer. He would reach into that bottomless satchel and produce a foot-long Foremost Kosher Salami, provided by a Warriors sponsor.

It turns out "The Zink" actually was a rassling announcer for promoter Ray Fabiani at the old Arena. On April 9, 1938, Matt Ring (a pseudonym for boxing writer Jack Fried) wrote this in the *Evening Bulletin*: "Brown hauled announcer Dave Zinkoff up on the ropes and hung him like a tailor's dummy . . ."

By then, the 1932 Temple University graduate had been the PA man for Owls football, basketball and boxing. Eddie Gottlieb hired him to be the announcer at Philadelphia SPHAs home games. That means "The Zink" not only introduced Harry Litwack, Hy Gotkin and Petey Rosenberg, but also Gil Fitch, whose orchestra played at the postgame dance in the Broadwood Hotel ballroom, a rococo house of foxtrots and two-handed set shots.

"Everybody was broke," Zink grinned one night at a long-forgotten game. "We had a wonderful time."

Three non-singing voices have become famous outside Philly: John Facenda, the NFL Films' "Voice of God"; Harry Kalas, voice of the Phillies and NFL highlights for HBO; and Dave Zinkoff. He died in 1985, at age 75.

He spent a lifetime informing stadium and arena crowds with his distinctively hokey style, ad-libbing always witty calls for the Owls, SPHAs, Harlem Globetrotters, Phillies, Warriors, 76ers, U.S. Pro Indoor Tennis Tournament and a list of lesser gigs longer than a Foremost Salami. He did it so well a banner in his honor hangs in the First Union Center rafters. Zinkoff Boulevard is named for him. He is one of the rare people with a nickname starting with *The*. The Big 5's outstanding rookie each season receives the Dave Zinkoff Award.

> ## I Remember
>
> One is the horrible thing that happened, don't remember where. There was a person lynched from a basketball standard. Left there as a sign. It was during the gang-fighting days. I didn't write about it [specifically], but referred to it in some stories. The other is seeing Elgin Baylor, wearing a big ol' overcoat, hat down over his head, walking into Convention Hall when he was coming in to play the Warriors. He was my idol. Remember seeing him coming out of the cold, his collar turned up, wide-brim hat. I had seen him play a few times on television, but that was the first time I got to see him in the flesh. He was a legend.
>
> *JOHN EDGAR WIDEMAN*
> *Philadelphia native and author*

My personal favorite of all "The Zink's" calls:

The Spectrum would be a third full, a boring three-set tennis match would be droning along, and you knew the announcement would come from Zinkoff any minute.

"Would the driver of the auto with Pennsylvania license plate number . . . please report immediately to the parking lot. Your lights are on, your doors are locked and your motor is running . . ."

The really big laugh would come about a half-hour later.

"To the driver of the auto with Pennsylvania license plate number . . . your doors are still locked. Your lights are no longer on. And . . . your motor has stopped running."

One man's other favorite calls

- "That was a pickle basket!" (Bill "Pickles" Kennedy)
- "By George!" (Jack George)
- "Gola Goal!" (Tom Gola)
- "Dipper Dunk!" (Wilt Chamberlain as Warrior)
- "Errrrrrrrrrrrrrrrrrrrrrrrrrrrrrving!" (Julius Erving)

— *Bill Conlin*

Can You Top These?

A list of favorite promotions through the years of former Sixers general manager Pat Williams

1. Little Arlene, who took on all comers in an eating contest
Williams: "Just as Bill Veeck had his midget, Little Arlene will always be part of my résumé. A dainty 95-pound lady who ate hot dog after hot dog, pizza after pizza, who drank soft drink after soft drink, then challenged anyone interested to an oyster-eating contest at Bookbinder's."

2. Victor the Bear
(My memory: In an unforgettable performance, Eagles special teams captain Vince Papale wrestled the bear at center court at halftime of a game. Papale explained his elaborate strategy of fakes and spins to a group of reporters before he went out, only to be warned, "Vince, that's a bear. That's not going to work." Victor back-pawed Papale across the face, leaving an ugly cut as people in the stands gasped.) Williams: "Victor made two appearances, once in '69 and again in the mid-'70s. I'll always have Little Arlene on one shoulder, Victor on the other. He left a big gash on the face of Vince Papale, and I was in fear that we had just done damage to an Eagles player."

3. Pepper the Singing Pig
Williams: "One headline the next day said 'Williams Has His Own Bay of Pigs Fiasco.' The fans booed, the pig relieved himself on the court."

4. God and Country Night
Williams: "Harold Katz had just bought the team in 1981. I broached the idea, he said to go ahead. We sold out. The next night, we were at a roast for Billy Cunningham, and Harold said, 'I'm as proud of you as if you were my own son.'"

5. Dick Allen and the Ebonistics
Williams: "You had to be there to understand the emotion from the fans toward Allen; he was so controversial. But he had a singing group, and their song was 'Echoes of November' on the Groovy Groove label. I can still hear him . . . 'I can still remember echoes of November . . .'"

6. The Don Nelson Coat-Throwing Contest
Williams: "In Milwaukee, he loses it, goes ballistic, heaves his coat. Like a glider, it fluttered over the court, like a big eagle. It had to have carried 40 feet. The next time the Bucks came to town, we had a coat-throwing contest to see who could throw it the farthest."

— Phil Jasner

Philly's Tallest and Shortest: By the Numbers

Name									
Todd MacCulloch	Eric Montross	Mel Counts	Benoit Benjamin	Eric Morgenthaler	Matt Geiger	Wilt Chamberlain	Dikembe Mutombo	Shawn Bradley	Manute Bol
Ht. 7-0	7-0	7-0	7-0	7-1	7-1	7-1	7-2	7-6	7-7
Seasons 1999–2001, 2002–	1997–98	1972–73	1997–99	1948–49	1998–2001	1959–62, 1964–68	2000–02	1993–95	1990–94

Name									
Greg Grant	Angelo Musi Jr.	Petey Rosenberg	Jerry Rullo	Kenny Sailors	Dana Barros	Scott Brooks	Speedy Claxton	Pickles Kennedy	Andre D. Turner
Ht. 5-7	5-9	5-10	5-10	5-10	5-11	5-11	5-11	5-11	5-11
Seasons 1991–93, 1995–96	1946–49	1946–47	1946–47, 1948–50	1947–48	1993–95	1988–90	2000–02	1960–61	1990–91

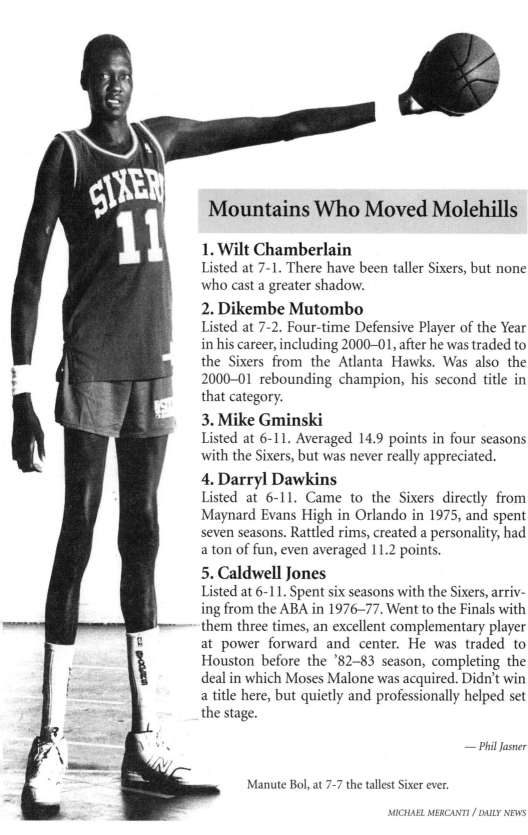

Mountains Who Moved Molehills

1. Wilt Chamberlain
Listed at 7-1. There have been taller Sixers, but none who cast a greater shadow.

2. Dikembe Mutombo
Listed at 7-2. Four-time Defensive Player of the Year in his career, including 2000–01, after he was traded to the Sixers from the Atlanta Hawks. Was also the 2000–01 rebounding champion, his second title in that category.

3. Mike Gminski
Listed at 6-11. Averaged 14.9 points in four seasons with the Sixers, but was never really appreciated.

4. Darryl Dawkins
Listed at 6-11. Came to the Sixers directly from Maynard Evans High in Orlando in 1975, and spent seven seasons. Rattled rims, created a personality, had a ton of fun, even averaged 11.2 points.

5. Caldwell Jones
Listed at 6-11. Spent six seasons with the Sixers, arriving from the ABA in 1976–77. Went to the Finals with them three times, an excellent complementary player at power forward and center. He was traded to Houston before the '82–83 season, completing the deal in which Moses Malone was acquired. Didn't win a title here, but quietly and professionally helped set the stage.

— *Phil Jasner*

Manute Bol, at 7-7 the tallest Sixer ever.

MICHAEL MERCANTI / DAILY NEWS

Franchise's Short but Sweetest

1. Allen Iverson
He's listed at 6 feet. But no one shows more heart and explosiveness.

2. Guy Rodgers
Also listed at 6 feet, but was just barely that. The best-ever Philadelphia guard.

3. Dana Barros
Then-coach John Lucas needed a workhorse, and found one in Barros, who admits to being about 5-11. In 1994–95, he averaged 20.6 points and 7.5 assists.

4. Angelo Musi
Listed at 5-9. Played 1946–47 through '48–49, averaging 8.4 points.

5. Scott Brooks
Listed at 5-11. Played the first two of a 10-season career with the Sixers. Made the team on sheer guts in 1988–89, survived on defense and an ability to knock down three-pointers.

Convention Hall, the Sixers' home before the Spectrum.

DAILY NEWS FILE PHOTO

Home Sweet Homes

The Philadelphia Warriors, born in 1946–47, almost didn't stay. And when they did, the legendary Eddie Gottlieb had to borrow $10,000 to make it happen.

That's the way Harvey Pollack remembers it. Pollack was with the Warriors in their inception in 1946–47, has served as a public relations director for both the Warriors and the 76ers, is currently the Sixers' director of statistical information and is recognized as a basketball historian.

There are now three generations of his family helping man the scorer's table crew for Sixers games at the First Union Center.

"We were 12–57 in 1952–53," Pollack recalled. "Walter Annenberg, who owned the team, folded his American Hockey League team, the Philadelphia Rockets, and would have folded the Warriors.

"But Gotty bought them for $25,000. He had to borrow $5,000 each from Lou Glazer and Jules Trumper. He moved the team from the Arena to Convention Hall. If he hadn't bought it, it would've gone down the tubes.

"That year, we played 30 home games, but only 17 were in Philly. If I remember correctly, we played games in Louisville, Baltimore and Raleigh, but I can't remember whether they were all designated as home games."

> ## I Remember
>
> [I] remember we had to beat St. Joe's one year to go to the NCAAs, it was late in the game, and [La Salle's] George Sutor tips the ball, catches it, shoots it, tips it, about four in a row, ends up grabbing the rim and it bent into a pretzel. Those days they didn't have them around to just roll in, so they got to get a ladder, put on a new rim. Game's delayed about a half-hour. We're in control of the game, but I remember Jimmy Lynam comes running by us, and says, "Let's go [huddle], coach [Ramsay] will tell us how to beat them." And they came back and won. I always looked at that, remember thinking what kind of confidence they had, the belief in themselves. It's a vivid memory in a positive way. We jump out, and what happens, but a truck hits us. I told Jimmy that story. I think he really believed [what he said]. I also know him well enough to know that he was probably trying to get into our heads.
>
> *BILL RAFTERY*
> *CBS Sports commentator*
> *La Salle University player (1960–63)*

The Warriors weren't exactly a cash cow. They frequently opened doubleheaders for the Harlem Globetrotters. If the 'Trotters were scheduled in Chicago or Pittsburgh or wherever, NBA games often preceded them. When the Warriors played home games in Pittsburgh, Pollack and his crew had to transport the necessary materials.

"We started out with five-sheet carbon-copy books that we got from the *Bulletin* to do the box scores," Pollack recalled. "Then we'd rewrite it, so we'd have 10 copies. We moved from there to ditto machines, mimeographs."

Times, Pollack said, have clearly changed. The Sixers have been setting attendance records for six seasons. Every home game in the 2001–02 season drew at least 20,000, a record.

A comparison: The Sixers acquired Wilt Chamberlain from San Francisco (the former Philadelphia Warriors) January 15, 1965, for Lee Shaffer, Connie Dierking, Paul Neumann and cash. Chamberlain made his home debut with his new team six days later.

The Sixers won, 111–102.

The game was at the Arena, at 46th and Market Streets.

The crowd was 6,140.

A sellout.

— *Phil Jasner*

Team Did Some Bouncing Around

These have been the primary home courts of the 76ers, who came to Philadelphia in 1963–64 from Syracuse, New York:

• Convention Hall, until 1967–68

• The Arena, for Wilt Chamberlain's homecoming vs. San Francisco, January 21, 1965

• The Spectrum (becoming the CoreStates Spectrum, now the First Union Spectrum), 1967–68 through '95–96

• The CoreStates Center (now the First Union Center) since '96–97

• The Palestra, one game and one playoff game, '67–68

But there have been other venues that have served as home courts for them, including:

1963–64

Scranton, Pennsylvania
Syracuse, New York
Yardley, Pennsylvania
Hershey, Pennsylvania

1964–65

Syracuse, five games
Pittsburgh, Pennsylvania
Tulsa, Oklahoma

1965–66

Syracuse, three games
Charleston, West Virginia
Greensboro, North Carolina
Pittsburgh

Wilt Chamberlain has a chat with the Celtics' Bill Russell.

I Remember

As a player, that Immaculata experience was just unbelievable. Of course, everyone got involved and it went on and on . . . and it still goes on. People will say, "I remember watching you play at Immaculata," or "My mother went to school with you."

As a coach, the Final Four [in 2000], just to wait that long to get to the Final Four and for it to happen in my hometown was unbelievable. Both my family and my husband's family still live there . . . so it cost me a fortune in tickets. I think I sent half of the Immaculata community there, but it was very, very special.

And then just as a Philly kid, the Big 5. Going to everything at the Palestra. We used to walk from St. Joe's, we'd dribble a basketball from school there. I mean, that was college entertainment. As just a person who grew up there, the Big 5 was a big part. I was sitting last night watching St. Joe's–Villanova from the Pavilion, and I turned to my husband and said, "Why isn't this game at the Palestra?"

RENE PORTLAND
Penn State women's basketball coach

1966–67
Pittsburgh, six games
Syracuse, two games

1968–69
Syracuse, three games

1971–72
Hershey, four games

1972–73
Pittsburgh, six games
Hershey, four games

1973–74
Hershey, four games
There were many home courts for the Warriors, who were part of Philadelphia from 1946–47 through '61–62, when the franchise moved to San Francisco.

The primary homes were the Arena and Convention Hall. But other home games were played at: Sayre Junior High; Camden Convention Hall; Hershey, Pennsylvania; Trenton, New Jersey; Collingswood, New Jersey; Abraham Lincoln High; Fallsington, Pennsylvania; Bethlehem, Pennsylvania; the Palestra; Saratoga Springs, New York; White Plains, New York; Albany, New York.

(These lists were compiled with the assistance of Harvey Pollack, the Sixers' director of statistical information.)

Ten Best from the Area

1. Wilt Chamberlain

31,419 points, 23,924 rebounds, 30.1 career scoring average, 118 games of 50 points or more, 15 of the top 20 scoring performances in NBA history, 14 of the top 24 rebounding performances. He always said, "Nobody loves Goliath." He'd be surprised.

2. Earl Monroe

Averaged 18.8 points in 13 seasons. If he didn't invent the spin move, he should get credit for it anyway. He was Magic before Magic.

3. Kobe Bryant

Remember all the critics who said he should have gone to college rather than directly from Lower Merion High to the pros? He has already won three championships with the Los Angeles Lakers.

Rasheed Wallace ranks on our list of top ten players.

DAILY NEWS FILE PHOTO

4. Paul Arizin

Averaged 22.8 points, 8.6 rebounds and 2.3 assists as a wheezing 6-4 forward with an impossible-to-duplicate flat jump shot. And he did it in 10 seasons, all with the Warriors.

5. Larry Foust

This is one that could have easily slipped through the cracks, because this 6-9 forward retired after the 1961–62 season after 12 seasons with Fort Wayne, Minneapolis and St. Louis. But he prepped at Southeast Catholic and La Salle for a career in which he averaged 13.7 points and 9.8 rebounds.

6. Guy Rodgers

Universally recognized as the best-ever guard from the area. Twice led the NBA in assists. He played four seasons in Philadelphia, then went west with the Warriors to San Francisco, where he is still that segment of the franchise's all-time assists leader with 4,855 from 1958–59 through 1965–66.

7. Tom Gola

His career stats of 11.3 points, 8.0 rebounds and 4.2 assists over 10 seasons, the first six with the Warriors, don't begin to show his value or impact. He was the kind of all-around player that current Sixers coach Larry Brown forever seeks.

8. Rasheed Wallace

The 2002–03 season will be his eighth in the NBA. Best known for his penchant for technical fouls and ejections. But at 6-11, he's as talented as virtually anyone in the league. If he ever manages his emotions better, he could climb on this list.

9. Geoff Petrie

He averaged 21.8 points in six seasons, going from Springfield (Delco) High to Princeton to the pros. I'll never forget fabled Plymouth-Whitemarsh High coach Henry Stofko watching him warm up for a high school game at St. Joseph's Fieldhouse and saying, "Someday he'll be a pro."

10. Wali Jones

Larry Costello went out with an injury, and he became the starting point guard for the 1966–67 champion Sixers. A relentless defender, an excellent passer with a jump shot that Billy Cunningham once described as looking "as if he were waving to everyone in the stands."

(This list was compiled with input from Sonny Hill, Jack Ramsay, John Nash, Jack Scheuer and others.)

— Phil Jasner

Baldy Was Giveaway Tip of the Iceberg

Giveaways have become a big deal for the Sixers and their fans.

Initially, they were a ploy on the part of the organization to sell seats. The Sixers had yet to jell into a contender and a so-so opponent would not be enough to bring in the fans.

Today, giveaways are no longer an incentive for fans to come out. Sellouts are a commonplace occurrence at the First Union, yet giveaways remain a staple of Sixers promotions people. Giveaways generate media, in part due to the fact that they have become prized as collectibles.

"We used to be able to judge [the success of a giveaway] by sheer numbers in attendance," said Lara White, the Sixers' senior vice president. "Now we gauge it by the enthusiasm it generates, the calls we get [from people saying]: 'Can I get one of those?'"

Giveaways have been used as promotional tools for years in sports, yet they caught on in a big way in Philadelphia just a few years ago. To help boost attendance for a game against Golden State in January 1998, Dave Coskey, the Sixers' executive vice president, came up with the idea of handing out a Beanie Baby, "Baldy the Eagle." Against an opponent that the year before drew just 10,932, the Sixers sold out the First Union Center. Said White, "It was a great way to get people through the door."

Other giveaways followed. Some of the more successful ones have included "The First Alien Iverson," "The Allen Iverson Bobble Head Doll" and "The Allen Iverson Celebriduck." To show how prized some of these items have become, the prototype for "The First Alien Iverson" sold on eBay for $900. The prototype for "The Allen Iverson Bobble Head" sold there for upwards of $300.

Also well received was "The Moses Malone Bobble Head Doll," which has become a collectible since it was passed out in honor of the Hall of Fame election of the former Sixers center.

Said Coskey, "Our aim is for this to be a fun experience and the giveaways just add to that."

— Mark Kram

I Remember

I think what struck me the most when I first came to the Greater Philadelphia area, coaching nine years at Lehigh University, was how the tradition is just ingrained into young players from an early age. It seemed like players there, especially Philadelphia Catholic League players, dream of growing up and playing in the Big 5, playing in the Palestra much the way kids in Nebraska grow up thinking of playing football for the Cornhuskers. It just seems like, if you're a young kid growing up in Philly, that's what everybody is destined to become, a Big 5 player or a player at the next level.

I've always thought it was a very provincial area, where the people who grow up there very seldom leave, more than most big cities. I think that's the reason that tradition has grown so strongly over the years.

BRIAN HILL
New Orleans Hornets assistant coach
Former coach, Lehigh University

Games for All Ages

The best single-game performances for Philadelphia players

1. Wilt Chamberlain's 100-point game
You were expecting maybe something else? Sorry, this is not the spot to go for an off-the-wall selection. On March 2, 1962, in the Warriors' 169–147 victory over the New York Knicks in Hershey, Pennsylvania, Chamberlain hit 36 of 63 field goals and, amazingly, 28 of 32 free throws to set a record that figures to stand forever.

2. Wilt's 55-rebound game
Not as celebrated as the 100-point outburst, this is another of Wilt's many NBA records that appears unbreakable. And it is even more notable because it came against the Boston Celtics and Wilt's fiercest rival, Bill Russell, on November 24, 1960, at Convention Hall. The Celtics, alas, won the game, 132–129.

3. Now, that's a triple-double
On February 2, 1968, Wilt posted 22 points, 25 rebounds and 21 assists — the most assists in one game ever dished out by a center — to lead the Sixers

to a victory over the Detroit Pistons at the Spectrum. No other NBA player has had a triple-double with 20 or more in each category.

4. Don't bring that mess in here

Blocked shots were not an official NBA statistic until the 1973–74 season, so Elmore Smith's 17 rejections for the Los Angeles Lakers on October 28, 1973, hold the top spot. Sixers publicist Harvey Pollack kept his own stats, however. He counted 25 rejection slips sent out by Wilt on November 26, 1959, in a 143–130 victory over the Celtics.

5. Fulks fills it up

Joe Fulks' feats are distant memories now, but he was a scoring machine for the Warriors in the early days of pro hoops. In a Basketball Association of America game against the Indianapolis Olympians on February 10, 1949, Fulks poured in 63 points — a record that stood until the Minneapolis Lakers' Elgin Baylor scored 64 on November 8, 1959.

— Bernard Fernandez

Freeze Frames

A look at the top five individual plays in Philadelphia pro basketball history

1. The sweetest scoop

It is the highlight that has been replayed so often it has become a part of our collective sports consciousness: Julius Erving going baseline against the Los Angeles Lakers in Game 4 of the 1980 NBA Finals. After floating behind the backboard all the way to the other side of the hoop, he put up a soft, under-handed scoop over the outstretched hand of Kareem Abdul-Jabbar. "My mouth just dropped open," said an incredulous Magic Johnson. "I thought, 'Should we take the ball out or should we ask him to do it again?'"

2. Doc cleared for takeoff

Of all the high fliers who have played here, Dr. J flew higher and more spectacularly than anyone. None of Erving's dunks, however, was more awesome than the take-off-from-the-foul-line, tomahawk slam he threw down over the Lakers' Michael Cooper in a January 1983 regular-season game.

The Lakers' Kobe Bryant is one of the area's best products.

DAILY NEWS FILE PHOTO

3. A.I. undresses M.J.

Allen Iverson's signature move is his killer crossover, which left the great Michael Jordan frozen in his tracks before tossing in a jumper in a March 18, 1997, game during Iverson's rookie season.

4. Long arm of the Dipper

Opponents knew not to challenge Wilt Chamberlain in the lane, but the San Francisco Warriors' Rick Barry thought he was safe when he attempted a long jumper in the closing seconds of Game 6 of the NBA Finals in 1967. Wrong. Wilt flew out from under the basket, achieved full extension and swatted away Barry's shot in the final minute to help preserve the 76ers' title-clinching, 125–122 victory.

5. Erving dials long distance

Sure, he was best known for his aerial antics, but Doc's hurried, buzzer-beating three-pointer under pressure at Dallas on February 28, 1986, gave the Sixers a 123–120 victory over the stunned Mavericks.

— Harvey Pollack, Bob Vetrone Sr. and Bernard Fernandez

Legendary Faces in the Sixers' Crowd

(in alphabetical order)

Bryan Abrams

Recognizable by his bald dome and flashy Versace threads, Abrams has held season tickets for 24 years and has missed just three home games. "And I only missed them because of deaths in the family," said Abrams, who says he has also attended games in every NBA city except Memphis. Abrams, who owns a ticket agency, says that "from November to June I eat, breathe and sleep Sixers." He is also one of the more vocal hecklers of opponents at the First Union Center.

Irv Block

When Block first purchased season tickets to the Warriors games in 1957, it cost him a total of $57. "Now that same seat that used to go for $2.25 goes for $475," said Block, who did not miss a single pro game in Philadelphia between 1957 and 1987. In fact, he attended an average of 100 pro games a year during that period. He was in Hershey, Pennsylvania, when Wilt Chamberlain scored 100 points in a game, and remembers a snowy evening in Philadelphia in the early 1960s when Chamberlain and his Warriors met the Bill Russell–led Celtics. "The building was packed and there were a thousand people outside on the sidewalk trying to get in," Block said. "It was before public transportation, and I remember we walked 30-some blocks in the cold to get there."

Joseph and Arlieen Franco

Having held season tickets since 1979, the Francos drive in from the Jersey shore to attend games, which is a $1^1/_2$–hour trip each way. Once, back in the early 1990s, Joe remembers that Sixers center Rick Mahorn exchanged shoes with his son, Paul, who just happened to have the same shoe size: 13. "Paul had on these Carolina blue Nikes, and Mahorn noticed them," said Franco. "He said, 'Those are ugly shoes!' He asked Paul what size he was, and said, 'I got to have them.' So he and Paul exchanged shoes and Mahorn checked into the game."

Karen McCaslin

Known by her nickname, "The Rose Princess," McCaslin has had season tickets for just two years but is a devoted fan who attends every home game. "The Princess" bought roses for the mothers and wives of each player during the Sixers-Lakers series in 2001, and wears a jersey autographed by dozens of players and celebrities. She drives in from Collegeville, Pennsylvania, for each game, which she says can take an hour or so, and also has season tickets to the Eagles and Phillies. Says McCaslin, "I just love going to the games."

Steve Solms

How big a fan is Solms? To begin with, he has held season tickets since 1962. And he even named his only son after 76ers Hall of Fame center Moses Malone. When Julius "Dr. J" Erving joined the Sixers in 1976–77 and was introduced to the Spectrum crowd for his first game, Solms walked out on the floor and handed him a doctor's bag.

— Mark Kram

More to history than Warriors, Sixers

The Warriors and the Sixers have played on the big stage of the NBA, but professional basketball in Philadelphia also has played off–Broad Street, in a manner of speaking.

Red Klotz was a member of the 1942–43 SPHAs (the acronym stood for South Philadelphia Hebrew Association), who won the championship of the old (read pre-NBA) American Basketball League with a team almost exclusively made up of local Jewish players.

"The team was owned by Eddie Gottlieb, who later owned the Warriors," recalled Klotz, perhaps best known as the longtime player-coach for the Washington Generals, perennial victims of the Harlem Globetrotters. "They won quite a few championships in the ABL."

Like the SPHAs before it, the Eastern League had a strong local presence in the 1950s and '60s with franchises, at various times, in Philadelphia, Camden and Wilmington. The level of basketball was not far off that being played in the NBA, according to Sonny Hill, who was a rookie with the Camden Bullets in 1958.

"When I broke in, there were eight teams in the NBA and eight teams in the Eastern League," Hill said. "Really, there were only 16 teams in the world where you could play and get paid.

"The Eastern League had guys who were involved in the [college point-shaving scandals] of the 1950s [and were barred from the NBA], but were great players. We had black players who were better than some in the NBA, but were denied the opportunity because of the racial quota system that was in place at that time.

"Bob Love [a longtime standout with the Chicago Bulls] is a great example of someone who played in the Eastern League and went on to become a major star in the NBA."

Not that anyone was getting rich playing in the Eastern League, Hill noted.

"There was more structure in the NBA because those guys, generally speaking, were full-time basketball players," he said. "In the Eastern League, we played a 28-game schedule with most of the games on weekends and holidays. Guys had jobs the rest of the week.

"When the Warriors moved to the West Coast [following the 1961–62 season], Paul Arizin decided he didn't want to go because he had a very good position here with IBM. He played in the Eastern League and I don't think he made more than $175 a game, even though he was voted one of the 50 greatest players in NBA history a few years ago."

The salary structure hadn't improved when the Wildwood Aces of the summer USBL moved to Philadelphia in 1987. The Aces played at Jake Nevin Field House and St. Joseph's Fieldhouse for two seasons, never quite finding an audience. Two other Philly-based USBL teams, the Spirit in 1991 and '92, and the Power in '97, also unsuccessfully attempted to make a go in a town whose fan base was more attuned to the major pro franchises.

— *Bernard Fernandez*

I Remember

For a basketball fan who's been raised near an intersection of Tobacco Road and bleeds Carolina blue, my wife looked at me quizzically when I told her I would be making a pilgrimage to see a college basketball tripleheader at Philadelphia's fabled Palestra in November.

"What's a Palestra?" she asked.

I tried to elaborate.

"It's like Cameron Indoor Stadium except that it's got more history and five teams have called it their home court at the same time."

"Oh, great," she said, not impressed. "Well, have fun."

I did. For a true hoops junkie, visiting the Palestra was like a walk to Mecca . . . The Palestra, with all its warmth, history and acoustics, embodies college basketball the way it ought to be. This is something truly special you have here. Six basketball-playing schools, one city, one wonderful arena. Even Tobacco Road, whose closest rivals are 10 miles apart, can't compete with that.

SCOTT SMITH
Managing editor, Street & Smith Sports Annuals

A View from the Outside

"Ordinary people playing an extraordinary game"

Phil Martelli was in San Diego in March 2001, a roomful of writers at his feet, an opportunity to crack a window to his world.

He was free-associating a bit, at least half-seriously, but he was quite heartfelt on one thing: "One thing I hate is when people call me 'Coach.' Don't 'Coach' me. If you're talking to me, I'm 'Phil.'"

Philadelphia basketball has always struck me that way. We're all human here.

Not that there haven't been great coaches, and great coaches with great egos, and the same with players, but nobody felt the need to hire bodyguards. Martelli, Jim Boyle, Jim Lynam, John Chaney, Don Casey, Speedy Morris and Lefty Ervin could talk to anybody. More importantly, they *would*.

Guys would coach in a Big 5 tripleheader at the Palestra and go straight to Cavanaugh's. In 1978, *Daily News* writer Dick "Hoops" Weiss got married somewhere in Delaware County, and three Big 5 coaches were there.

One reason Villanova came to be resented by the fans of the Other 4 was that Villanova went "uptown," into the Big East, and rarely recruited city kids. The tall poppy syndrome, as the Australians say. Still, the Wildcats were frat brothers, albeit on probation, and the city had no trouble celebrating the great '85 NCAA run — and the last college game without a three-point line. As Chaney said, "That Rollie Massimino, he could get butter from a duck."

Perhaps it's oversimplifying, but New York basketball was about individuals. Philadelphia had them, too, but it was mostly about teams, defense, playing together, playing in observance of a "right way" that was hard to define but easy to spot. A kid could score five points, do everything else well, and impress more people in Philly than anywhere else.

People call Philly a "basketball town," which it is, but they need to be more specific. It is a great basketball-playing, basketball-talking, basketball-thinking town. It is not a great basketball-watching town. In 1981, the 76ers played Milwaukee in the Eastern finals and drew 6,074 in an 18,276-seat Spectrum. It was Easter, explained Pat Williams — which must have meant there were 30,000 Hindus across the street, watching the Phillies and the Cubs. When I came to Philly in 1978 I expected a sold-out Palestra every night, and was disappointed. The Sixers now fill their new arena, but only through a herculean marketing campaign. I doubt if any athlete as great as Julius Erving ever performed before a lower percentage of capacity, at home.

That bothered the owners, and occasionally the players, but it really was a footnote. Those who did show up knew what they were watching. Basketball crowds didn't seem nearly as petulant as Eagle and Phillie crowds were. There was no overwhelming imperative to get as drunk as one possibly could. There was a game to watch.

The Sixers have been many different things, of course, but even they managed a common touch for many years. No moment was warmer than Grover Washington Jr. showing up for the big games, putting his signature on the national anthem and then nodding and smiling at Doc. Or the Celtic games, the ones that would sell out the Spectrum weeks in advance, when Erving and Maurice Cheeks and Andrew Toney would put something together, and Bill Fitch would stand up and call a disgusted timeout, and above the crowd you could hear the glorious growl of Dave Zinkoff at the mike: "Boston calls TIIIIIIIIIME!"

When the Sixers won their '83 title with help from a Hessian named Moses Malone, all the people who would never pay to watch the NBA in January elbowed their way into Veterans Stadium for the celebration. Yes, they were lured by a winner, but they saw the ambassadorial Erving, the earnest Bobby Jones. These were ordinary people who played an extraordinary game, and in that way they lived for the city.

— Mark Whicker
Orange County Register

Wilt Chamberlain

DAILY NEWS FILE PHOTO

Chapter Three
The Collegians

A Culture Enveloped by History, Reinvigorated by the Senses

DICK JERARDI

College basketball in this city is a feeling. You can't see it on television. You can't hear it on radio. You can't be told about it. You need to be there.

You must be inside the Palestra on a cold January night a few minutes before two city teams play. You have to be at the St. Joe's Fieldhouse when the Hawks are one victory away from a conference title. You must have seen a game at the old Cat House on Lancaster Avenue. You needed to attend the old Quaker City Tournament. You need to know the difference between a streamer and a rollout. Then, you understand.

There are the two national championships (La Salle, 1954, and Villanova, 1985), the nine Final Fours (Villanova three times, La Salle and Temple twice each, Penn and St. Joe's once each), the four Hall of Fame coaches (Penn's Chuck Daly, St. Joe's Jack Ramsay and Temple's John Chaney and Harry Litwack), the two Hall of Fame players (La Salle's Tom Gola, Villanova's Paul Arizin), the five national players of the year (Arizin, St. Joe's George Senesky and La Salle's Gola, Michael Brooks and Lionel Simmons) and the great single-season scorers (Arizin, Senesky, Temple's Bill Mlkvy and La Salle's Randy Woods).

There is the unmatched artistry of La Salle's Ken Durrett, the unparalleled ballhandling of Temple's Guy Rodgers and the how-good-were-they memories of the 1968–69 La Salle team that never got an NCAA Tournament chance because of the sins of a prior coach.

There is all that. And there is just this feeling.

It can't be explained by reading about it. It can't be understood by asking questions. Old films don't really illuminate it.

It helps a little to walk around the Palestra a few dozen times, savoring the walls that are adorned with the building's history.

Gathering around coach Rollie Massimino during Villanova's victory parade in 1985 are (from left) R.C. Massimino, Ed Pinckney, Wyatt Maker, Chuck Everson, Dwight Wilbur, Veltra Dawson and Brian Harrington.

DAILY NEWS FILE PHOTO

Still, trying to explain why we love the game so is like explaining why we like to breathe. We just do.

In the 1960s and '70s, heyday of the Big 5, the teams were so embraced because so many people knew the players so intimately for so long. Many of the greatest Big 5 players of that era had played in the Public League and the Catholic League. By the time they were near graduation, it was as if they were part of the family.

Times, of course, have changed. No longer do this city's players rule this city's game. College basketball has gone from a regional sport to a national sport, a radio game to a television game.

Still, the feeling persists. Sit down in a gym on game night and close your eyes. Take in the pregame sounds and the smells. Imagine what it's going to be like when 10 players, three officials and a coach or two take over the court.

Enjoy the contest. Watch the scoreboard. Question calls. Question coaches.

Stick around for a while when it's over. Savor what you've seen. Watch the building slowly empty out. Walk very slowly to the exits when it does.

When you're there, you see it, you hear it, and you understand it. You get the feeling.

We Interrupt This Game

Bomb scare

Everyone left the building. Everyone, that is, but Les Keiter and his Channel 17 viewing audience.

It was halftime of Villanova–St. Joseph's on February 20, 1965, and 9,000-plus people were being asked to leave the Palestra due to a bomb scare. Keiter was told to stay in the broadcast booth high above the court through the entire ordeal by his station manager (who was, quite conveniently, back at the station).

After about a 30-minute delay and searches through coats and hats by police and officials, the players and coaches (who went next door to Hutchinson Gym) and fans (who were sent outdoors, where it was 27 degrees) rejoined Keiter, and the Hawks held on, 69–61.

The tip was everything

Citing weather and travel problems on Friday, January 12, 1996, 18th-ranked Arizona canceled a Saturday afternoon game with St. Joseph's at the Palestra. The cancellation came just 48 hours after the Hawks took top-ranked Massachusetts to overtime. (Arizona officials failed to cite that game publicly.)

The Hawks trudged through 52-degree conditions to take the Palestra court for what would have been the opening tap. They won the tap, but it just didn't seem the same.

Ballooning to 3,000

It was February 22, 1989, and 15 feet of Civic Center hardwood is all that stood between La Salle's Lionel Simmons and immortality, which is what becoming the fifth NCAA Division I player to reach 3,000 points will get you.

> ### I Remember
>
> The first thing that comes to mind is a bitter-cold winter night . . . finding a parking place somewhere at the University of Pennsylvania campus. Pulling a Navy pea jacket up over your neck . . . and leaning into the wind to seek warmth and comfort at the Palestra. And the first thing that hits you is the smell . . . a combination of decades of sweat and perspiration . . . and then four hours of frenzy, Philadelphia frenzy. That's my very earliest memory. Those doubleheaders. You might catch a Big 5 game or might catch Cincinnati, Dayton, NC State, Kansas. Of course, the memory that's most important to me, riding down an open flat-bedded truck, right down Broad Street, a warm June morning, with untold thousands, maybe millions, lining the street, celebrating a team championship that had been a long time coming. That's a moment you dream about, you long for. It was almost surreal, almost like it didn't happen . . . but it did.
>
> *PAT WILLIAMS*
> *Orlando Magic senior vice president*
> *Former Sixers general manager*

It was on a free throw 7 minutes, 16 seconds into the game, and when he made it, balloons descended from the ceiling. As that happened, Simmons was lifted to his teammates' shoulders, his mother joined him for an on-court hug and a commemorative ball was presented in front of 8,136 thankful fans.

After about 10 minutes, they resumed what passed for a game that night, as the Explorers pounded a Steve Lappas–coached Manhattan team, 100–60.

Third for nothing

Following the assassination attempt on President Reagan's life on March 30, 1981, the NCAA Basketball Committee waited until almost 8 p.m. to decide whether to play the NCAA title game between Indiana and North Carolina at the Spectrum.

A since-halted trademark of the Palestra was a shower of streamers, prompted by the game's first basket.

DAILY NEWS FILE PHOTO

But LSU and Virginia had little choice but to suit up for the 5 p.m. consolation game, which went on without any thought of a cancellation or postponement. The Cavaliers prevailed, 78–74, in front of about 8,000.

When they finally decided to play the championship game, Isiah Thomas and the Hoosiers topped North Carolina, 63–50.

Three and a half months later, the NCAA disbanded the third-place game, a tournament staple since 1946.

Streamers

They made the beginnings of Palestra games as eagerly anticipated as the endings. So what if a few people with brooms had to spend 90 seconds cleaning the court? At least the coaches got a chance to do a little more coaching early on.

It was pageantry, it was tradition, it was beautiful.

It was cool!

— *Bob Vetrone Jr.*

Contemporary Slamma Jammers

Tim Thomas, Villanova
Set the stage in the third game of his career against Tulane in Puerto Rico when he seemed to take off from halfcourt.

Eddie Jones, Temple
Of all of the guys who could sky, Jones was the most explosive.

Kerry Kittles, Villanova
Nobody in the Big 5 could elevate like Kittles.

Mark Bass, St. Joe's
Anyone who's listed at a generous 5-9 and can get to the rim with authority deserves a mention.

Ugonna Onyekwe, Penn
The ambidextrous Quaker can come at you from both sides.

— Dana Pennett O'Neil

Five Classics to Savor

Both are Big 5 Hall of Famers. Only the walls of the Palestra have seen more college basketball in this city.

Ask legendary writer/broadcaster/sports information director Bob Vetrone and *Associated Press* reporter Jack Scheuer to recall their best memories of area college basketball and it is like opening a hoops vault. Their memories pour out, as crystal clear and precise as the day the game was played. They've seen all the great players, witnessed all the magic that is the Big 5.

It's not easy to whittle down their favorites. There are too many memorable games to recall. So calling these the best Philadelphia college basketball games is too subjective. Let's just say these are a handful that really stand out, plus a bonus match that didn't include Philly teams but earns a note of distinction just the same.

> ### I Remember
>
> I met Sonny Hill when I was [playing] with St. Louis. He and I developed a real special relationship. You're going back 30-some years, when he was on TV. But that whole Baker League thing that he took over and then ran with, it was really special.
>
> The most special thing about Philadelphia basketball was when I came in with Creighton and played La Salle [December 1, 1962]. I got 35 rebounds in the Palestra and kicked their butts real good [91–72].
>
> *PAUL SILAS*
> *New Orleans Hornets head coach*

1. The bomb-scare game.

That's all anyone calls it. That's all anyone remembers. St. Joseph's vs. Villanova at the Palestra, February 20, 1965. Someone phoned in a bomb scare and the old gym was emptied, save for one person. That's what both Vetrone and Scheuer remember, that Channel 17 broadcaster Les Keiter, play-by-play announcer for the Big 5, stayed in the building to report on the scare. Eventually the threat was deemed a hoax and the fans returned. St. Joe's went on to win, 69–61, but the game took a back seat to Keiter's legend.

2. La Salle 101, Florida State 100, February 23, 1989, the Palestra.

Time was the only thing the Seminoles didn't have enough of. After trailing by 17 at the half, Florida State scored an absurd 67 points in the second half to make it a ballgame, and Tharon Mayes' putback of a rebound made it a one-point game just as time expired. Lionel Simmons finished with 36.

3. St. Joe's 71, Villanova 69, January 16, 1966, the Palestra.

The Hawks were ranked fifth in the country and would go on to the East Regionals of the NCAA Tournament. The Wildcats came into the game a lowly 5–7. Still, the Wildcats led almost the whole way and St. Joe's looked dead in the water when sharpshooter Billy Oakes fouled out. Except Big 5 magic was at work. Coach Jack Ramsay inserted seldom-used Steve Donches. Naturally, Donches sank the winning bucket from inside half-court along the sideline.

Bob Vetrone   Jack Scheuer

SCHEUER PHOTO:
JENNIFER MIDBERRY / DAILY NEWS

4. Loyola Marymount 99, St. Joe's 96, January 4, 1990, the Fieldhouse.

In Hank Gathers' homecoming to Philadelphia, Bo Kimble won the game on a 35-footer. Two months later, Gathers was dead and Kimble memorialized him with a lefthanded foul shot during the NCAA Tournament.

5. La Salle 74, Villanova 67, February 8, 1969.

Considered the city's best team of all time, the Explorers would go on to finish 23–1, but because of NCAA probation stemming from the regime of former coach Jim Harding, Tom Gola's bunch never got the recognition it deserved. This game earns its nod for the sheer talent on the floor at one time. La Salle brought Ken Durrett and the Wildcats countered with Howard Porter. It doesn't get much better.

Bonus: Duke 104, Kentucky 103, OT, March 28, 1992, the Spectrum, NCAA Tournament East Regional.
It didn't involve Philadelphia teams, but as Scheuer explained, "It's the best game I've ever seen in Philadelphia . . . which is saying a lot." Christian Laettner, 10-for-10 in the game, caught an improbable baseball pass, turned and sank a jumper at the top of the key at the buzzer to lift the favorite Blue Devils over the Wildcats and ultimately to their second consecutive national championship.

— Dana Pennett O'Neil

Greatest of the Non–Big 5 Upsets

1. Villanova 66, Georgetown 64
April 1, 1985: Playing for the 1985 NCAA championship in Lexington, Kentucky, Villanova played a nearly perfect game to beat top-ranked Georgetown and pull off the grand-daddy of all upsets.

Mighty Georgetown (35–3) was the defending NCAA champion and had just blasted St. John's in the national semifinals. Upstart Villanova came into the tournament with a modest 19–10 record, but got hot at the right time.

The Wildcats beat Memphis State in the Final Four to earn a third shot at Georgetown.

Incredibly, 'Nova sank 22 of 28 field goals against Georgetown, including nine of 10 in the second half. Dwayne McClain (17 points), Ed Pinckney (16), Harold Jensen (14) and Harold Pressley (11) all scored in double digits for the Wildcats.

1985 champions Ed Pinckney and Gary McLain

DAILY NEWS FILE PHOTO

2. Temple 60, Kentucky 59
December 20, 1947: Temple finished just 12–11, but its season was highlighted by a victory over the eventual NCAA champion Wildcats at Convention Hall. Ed Lerner scored 22 for Temple. UK's only other NCAA loss that season was to Notre Dame. Kentucky finished 36–3, losing to AAU champion Phillips Oil in the U.S. Olympic Trials, but later went on to beat France for the gold medal at the 1948 Olympics in London.

The Big 5 coaching lineup in 1970 (second from left): La Salle's Paul Westhead, St. Joseph's Jack McKinney, Penn's Dick Harter, Villanova's Jack Kraft and Temple's Harry Litwack.

DAILY NEWS FILE PHOTO

3. St. Joseph's 49, DePaul 48

March 13, 1981: The ninth-seeded Hawks (25–8) upset No. 1 overall seed DePaul in the NCAA Tournament. Blue Demons guard Skip Dillard missed the first of a one-and-one with 13 seconds left. The Hawks rebounded and Bryan Warrick pushed the ball up the court to Lonnie McFarlan, who passed from the right corner to John Smith under the basket. Smith made a wide-open layup to win as time expired. The Hawks' defense held DePaul stars Mark Aguirre and Terry Cummings to 14 combined points. DePaul finished 27–2.

4. Penn 72, North Carolina 71

March 11, 1979: In Raleigh, North Carolina, Tony Price had 25 points and nine rebounds and Ken Hall sank two free throws with 17 seconds left as the ninth-seeded Quakers (25–7) shocked ACC champion North Carolina (23–6) in an NCAA second-round game. Penn rode the upset wave all the way to the Final Four.

5. Villanova 59, Michigan 55

March 17, 1985: The Wildcats earned their invitation to the Sweet 16 by beating the Wolverines, the country's second-ranked team. Villanova secured its lead with a flawless delay game over the final $3^1/_2$ minutes, making 13 of 16 free throws. Dwayne McClain led the Wildcats with 20 points.

6. La Salle 75, Dayton 64

March 15, 1952: From the 1930s to the mid-1950s, the National Invitational Tournament was considered on par with or better than the NCAAs. The unseeded Explorers entered the tournament with a 19–5 record and upset Seton Hall, St. John's and Duquense to reach the finals. Freshman Tom Gola scored 22 and Norm Grekin 15 to lead the Explorers past favored Dayton (28–5) at Madison Square Garden.

I Remember

The cradle of the United States is Philadelphia, and the cradle of college basketball is Philadelphia with the Penn Palestra. They've just had some great players come out of that city, and at one time college basketball there — with the doubleheaders and tripleheaders and games on TV every night — was amazing.

PETE CARRIL
Sacramento Kings assistant coach
Former Princeton coach

7. Drexel 75, Memphis 63

March 14, 1996: Playing with a sprained ankle, Malik Rose still dominated with 21 points and 15 rebounds as the 12th-seeded Dragons posted their only NCAA Tournament victory by beating the No. 5 Tigers. Jeff Meyers (15), Mike DeRocckis (14), Chuck Guittar (10) and Cornelius Overby (10) all scored in double digits.

8. Penn 90, Nebraska 80

March 17, 1994: Barry Pierce hit 11 of 15 shots and scored 25 as the 11th-seeded Quakers gave the Ivy League its first NCAA victory in 11 seasons by upsetting the Big 8 champion and sixth-seeded Huskers.

9. Temple 74, Kansas 66, OT

December 22, 1995: In the Jimmy V Classic at the Meadowlands Arena, the Owls — with Marc Jackson, Levan Alston and Derrick Battie — defeated top-ranked Kansas. A week earlier, Temple had upset No. 2 Villanova.

10. Villanova 64, Connecticut 63

February 15, 1994: Kerry Kittles scored 24 and the Wildcats withstood a 24-point effort by Donyell Marshall to beat top-ranked UConn (29–5) at the Pavilion. The momentum carried Villanova (20–12) to the 1994 NIT title.

— John Smallwood

One Man's Favorites

20 Best Players

Drexel (2): Michael Anderson (1984–88); Malik Rose (1992–96)
La Salle (5): Michael Brooks (1976–80); Larry Cannon (1966–69); Ken Durrett (1968–71); Tom Gola (1951–55); Lionel Simmons (1986–90)
Penn (2): Ernie Beck (1950–53); Corky Calhoun (1969–72)
St. Joe's (2): Cliff Anderson (1964–67); Mike Bantom (1970–73)
Temple (4): Hal Lear (1953–56); Mark Macon (1987–91); Bill Mlkvy (1950–52); Guy Rodgers (1955–58)
Villanova (5): Paul Arizin (1947–50); Wali Jones (1961–64); Kerry Kittles (1992–96); John Pinone (1979–83); Howard Porter (1968–71)

10 Best Coaches

La Salle (1): Ken Loeffler (1949–55)
Penn (2): Chuck Daly (1971–77); Fran Dunphy (1989–present)
Philadelphia University (1): Herb Magee (1967–present)
St. Joe's (1): Jack Ramsay (1955–66)
Temple (3): John Chaney (1982–present); Harry Litwack (1952–73); Jimmy Usilton Sr. (1926–39)
Villanova (2): Jack Kraft (1961–73); Rollie Massimino (1973–92)

25 Best Teams
Drexel (1): 1995–96 (27–4)
La Salle (4): 1953–54 (26–4); 1954–55 (26–5); 1968–69 (23–1); 1989–90 (30–2)
Penn (5): 1952–53 (22–5); 1969–70 (25–2); 1970–71 (28–1); 1971–72 (25–3); 1993–94 (25–3)
St. Joe's (5): 1960–61 (25–5); 1964–65 (26–3); 1965–66 (24–5); 1985–86 (26–6); 1996–97 (26–7)
Temple (5): 1937–38 (23–2); 1955–56 (27–4); 1957–58 (27–3); 1986–87 (32–4); 1987–88 (32–2)
Villanova (5): 1938–39 (20–5); 1963–64 (24–4); 1970–71 (23–6); 1984–85 (25–10); 1994–95 (25–8)

— Dick Jerardi

Top 10 College Teams to Visit Philadelphia

A list of the best quintets to come to the city and play against one of the Big 5 teams

1. Kentucky
December 20, 1947
The legendary Adolph Rupp brought what would be his first NCAA championship team to Philadelphia and was upset, 60–59, by Temple. With All-Americas Alex Groza and Ralph Beard, UK finished 36–3 and in addition to the NCAA title won the 1948 Olympic gold medal, posting an 8–0 record. The Wildcats repeated as 1949 NCAA champs and went 68–5 in those two seasons.

2. Georgetown
February 15, 1984
Led by All-Americas Patrick Ewing and Reggie Williams, the Hoyas avenged an earlier loss to Villanova with a 59–46 victory at the Spectrum. Georgetown finished 34–3 and won the NCAA title.

Three visits to Philadelphia in 1996 netted Marcus Camby and Massachusetts two victories over Temple and one over St. Joe's.

GEORGE REYNOLDS / DAILY NEWS

3. UNLV
January 13, 1990
With future NBA first-round picks Stacey Augmon, Larry Johnson and Greg Anthony, the Runnin' Rebels edged Temple, 82–76, at the Spectrum. UNLV finished 35–5 and crushed Duke, 103–73, for the NCAA title. The Rebels went 34–1 the next season, losing in the Final Four to Duke.

4. Massachusetts
January 10, February 1, March 9, 1996
The No. 1 Minutemen came to Philadelphia and beat St. Joseph's, 94–89, and Temple, 59–35 and 75–61. UMass finished 35–2, losing in the Final Four to NCAA champion Kentucky.

5. Kentucky
February 8, 1998
On the way to their second NCAA title and third straight NCAA championship-game appearance, the Wildcats (35–4) took out Villanova, 79–63, at the First Union Center.

6. Wyoming
December 26, 1942
On the day after Christmas, the Cowboys crushed La Salle, 56–32, at Convention Hall. Wyoming finished 31–2 and beat St. John's for the 1943 NCAA title.

7. Duke
December 2, 2000
With player of the year Shane Battier and All-America Jason Williams, the Blue Devils buried a Temple team that made it to the Elite Eight. The Blue Devils won, 93–68, at the First Union Center. Duke finished 35–4 and won the NCAA title.

8. Indiana
December 28, 1939
Hall of Fame coach Branch McCracken brought the Hoosiers to the Main Line and defeated Villanova, 45–33. Indiana finished 20–3 and went on to win the 1940 NCAA title. Villanova (17–2) lost just one other game.

9. Georgetown
January 12, 1985
The 1984 NCAA champions earned a 52–50 victory over Villanova at the Spectrum. The 'Cats' victory over the 35–3 Hoyas for the 1985 NCAA title is one of the greatest upsets ever. This Hoyas nucleus went 69–6 over two seasons.

10. Duke
January 13, 1986
A Duke team that featured stars Johnny Dawkins, Tommy Amaker and Mark Alarie came to the Palestra and whipped St. Joe's, 87–66. Duke finished 37–3, losing the NCAA championship game to Louisville.

— *John Smallwood*

Rollouts That Left an Impression

This was unfurled at a Catholic League opening-round playoff game in the early '70s:

> *"Due to Catholic League Rules, No Rollouts Will Be*
> *Permitted at the Palestra"*

During one of the seasons in the mid-'70s when Keith and/or Larry and/or Reggie Herron was at Villanova, St. Joseph's fans pointed out that:

> *"Rollie is a Herron addict"*

Villanova fans once equated:

> *"Baboon + Drum = St. Joe Band"*

When Temple played an all-white South Carolina team in the early '60s:

> *"Owls knock Gamecocks black and blue — well blue anyway"*

In January of 1972, nine months after Villanova clocked Penn, 90–47, in the East Regional finals to advance to the Final Four in Houston, Penn rolled out a classless classic about Chris Ford, which we won't reprint here … But the Villanova fans had a response:

> *"What did you do with your Astrodome tickets?"*

After Villanova's participation in that Final Four was vacated, Penn volleyed again:

> *"Howard Porter Did Not Sign …*
> *"A Professional Contract …*
> *"Someone Forged His X … "*

Penn fans didn't save all of their venom in 1972 for Villanova, though:

> *"Hey Princeton: Good Luck … in the NIT"*

And the Quakers fans even took them on the road, as this one was unfurled during a tournament in Rochester, New York:

> *"Gantt Can't Decode Morse"*

And when Villanova entered a late-season game with three losses, two to Big 5 opponents, they were met with this:

> *"Villanova …*
> *"No. 2 in the Country,*
> *"No. 4 in the City"*

— Bob Vetrone Jr.

Evolution of the Philly Guard

The phenomenon of the Philly guard dates back to the 1950s, and became recognized nationally as a synonym for backcourt excellence. A badge of honor, if you will. There was no higher compliment. A Philly guard wasn't necessarily the best player on the floor or the most talented, although he could be. But a Philly guard was the most heady player out there. Most of the time, he had the ball in his hands. He was in control of whatever was happening. He relied on guile as much as pure skill. He was a leader, who always seemed to make the right play at the right time. The smart play.

He was everything you wanted a guard to be, and then some. He wasn't interested in making the highlight reels. He just wanted to make his team win. All could trace their roots to this city's Public or Catholic leagues. But it didn't start with one team, or one name. It just sort of evolved, a process that's ongoing. Only gym rats need apply. Sometimes it even applies to those who never saw a soft pretzel until college. Problem is, you could make this list three times longer and still not include everyone who probably belongs.

— Mike Kern

Guy Rodgers

Top "Philly" Guards

Guy Rodgers, Temple
(1955–58)
So, why isn't he in the Basketball Hall of Fame?

Jimmy Lynam, St. Joseph's
(1960–63)
One of the first consummate point men.

Jim O'Brien, St. Joseph's
(1971–74)
Solid, not flashy. Never lost the ball.

Steve Courtin, St. Joseph's
(1961–64)
Still the only Hawk to score 30 points in consecutive postseason games.

Steve Bilsky/Dave Wohl, Penn
(1968–71)
Interchangeable parts were largely responsible for program's emergence.

Fran O'Hanlon, Villanova
(1967–70)
As tough as they came, could shoot the ball.

Jerome Allen/Matt Maloney, Penn
(1992–95)
Another interchangeable combo, with maybe even more ways to beat you.

Howie Evans, Temple
(1984–88)
His 20-assist, single-turnover game vs. Villanova as a senior still stands out.

Matt Guokas, St. Joseph's
(1963–66)
First of the big (6-5) point guards.

Wali Jones
(1961–64)
Had no weaknesses, could control a game by shooting or conducting.

Doug Overton, La Salle
(1987–91)
Was just as important to those great teams as L-Train.

Rick Brunson, Temple
(1991–95)
As a senior, took the Owls to the NCAAs almost by himself.

Pepe Sanchez, Temple
(1996–2000)
Totally changed his game to embrace it through John Chaney's unique eyes.

— Mike Kern

Bilsky: Every Team Had Great Guards

When Steve Bilsky showed up in the Palestra to play in Dick Harter's Penn backcourt, he was certain about two things: the sun would rise east of the Schuylkill each morning and New York City guards were better than Philly guards.

The slick little point guard who would team with jump-shooting Dave Wohl to become one of the storied backcourts in the Golden Age of the Big 5 soon discovered he was working in the home office for college guard play.

"Everybody either had a great backcourt duo, or one outstanding guard," Penn's athletic director said in a recent interview.

When Bilsky and Wohl took over the controls in 1968–69, the Big 5 had reached its pinnacle of national prominence and influence. La Salle was ranked No. 2 in the nation with a team on probation for the sins of the coach who preceded Tom Gola.

"Bernie Williams and Fatty Taylor was a great backcourt," Bilsky said.

I asked Bilsky to distill the essence of the Big 5 guards he competed against. "Heady. They always knew how to play and always had a sense of the game and their team," he said.

During his years in the Big 5, Villanova and Penn both went deep into the NCAA tourney, Temple won an NIT title and La Salle would have given UCLA a run with a lineup led by brilliant Ken Durrett and charismatic Larry Cannon. The Wildcats eventually did give them a run, losing 68–62 in the 1971 title game.

Bilsky recalled one of his career's most bizarre games, a 32–30 victory on January 15, 1969.

"We played pure man-to-man, Villanova played that matchup zone," Bilsky said. "They had a great backcourt in Tommy Ingelsby and Chris Ford. We wanted to force them out of the zone."

With Bilsky and Wohl patiently dribbling around the perimeter and the Quakers taking only the surest of shots, Penn played a game of stallball that infuriated Villanova fans in the Palestra. "It was something like 13–12 at the half. I hit the jumper that beat them," Bilsky said.

> ## I Remember
>
> When I think of Philadelphia basketball, I'll always think of the Palestra, because that's where I grew up. I used to take the bus and the El into West Philadelphia every Wednesday and Saturday night to watch Big 5 doubleheaders with five, six kids from St. Bernadette's CYO. We used to pay $3 to sit in the west stands.
>
> I missed Guy [Rodgers] and Hal Lear of Temple — the best backcourt ever to play in the city. They were a little before my time. But I got a chance to experience the Big 5 in all of its glory from 1961 through 1972 … It was the golden era in Big 5 basketball and I feel privileged to have felt a part of it, both as a fan and as a sports writer. It's probably the biggest reason I got into this profession.
>
> *DICK WEISS*
> *New York Daily News*
> *Formerly of the Philadelphia Daily News*

The collegial atmosphere that prevailed in the Big 5 of that era was eroded by the animosity that erupted between Harter and Jack Kraft. Looking back, I view the fallout from that controversial game as the first tear in the fabric of an ex-officio basketball conference that was the nation's envy.

The Quakers were 28–0 and No. 2 in the polls when they met the Wildcats in the Eastern Regional final in 1971. Villanova unleashed a furious onslaught of power basketball, pressing 90 feet and running at every opportunity. The Wildcats' 90–47 victory shocked the East.

"They totally destroyed us," Bilsky said. "And that was the one year UCLA was a little vulnerable. They were in between great centers."

— *Bill Conlin*

Best Backcourts

Guy Rodgers and Hal Lear, *Temple*
(1955–56)
Still the standard. Could simply do it all.

Guy Rodgers and Bill "Pickles" Kennedy, *Temple*
(1957–58)
Also took the Owls to a Final Four.

Matt Guokas and Billy Oakes, *St. Joseph's*
(1964–66)
Complemented each other to perfection.

Dave Wohl and Steve Bilsky, *Penn*
(1968–71)
Hard to believe neither made all–Big 5. As seniors, backbone of one of the city's best teams.

Nate Blackwell and Howie Evans, *Temple*
(1983–87)
Blank brothers put up some serious numbers, ushered in the John Chaney era.

Larry Cannon, Roland "Fatty" Taylor and Bernie Williams, *La Salle*
(1967–69)
Provided great defense and pure shooting, for what many feel was the best team in city history.

Howie Evans and Mark Macon, *Temple*
(1987–88)
Made up backcourt for team that was ranked No. 1 in the country throughout the season.

Doug Overton and Randy Woods, *La Salle*
(1989–91)
Very underrated force, because of Lionel Simmons.

Chris Ford and Tom Ingelsby, *Villanova*
(1970–72)
Overshadowed by Howard Porter, helped take Wildcats to final game in 1971.

Wali Jones and George Leftwich, *Villanova*
(1961–63)
Flashy, distinctive point man and a deadly sniper.

Matt Maloney (12), watching teammate Barry Pierce fight Temple's Eddie Jones for the ball, never lost an Ivy League game during his career.

GEORGE REYNOLDS / DAILY NEWS

Matt Maloney and Jerome Allen, *Penn*
(1992–95)
Never lost an Ivy League game together (42–0).

Kerry Kittles and Alvin Williams, *Villanova*
(1993–96)
Just check the numbers. They don't lie.

— Mike Kern

All-Time One-Man Shows in a Season

George Senesky, *St. Joe's*
(1942–43)
Averaged 23.4 points on a team that scored just 56.3 points per game. Next-highest scorer averaged 8.9 points. Team was 18–4.

Bill Mlkvy, *Temple*
(1950–51)
Averaged 29.2 points, the most in one season by any player in city history. Scored 73 points in the season finale against Wilkes College. Team finished 12–13.

Tom Gola, *La Salle*
(1953–54)
Scored 690 points and had 652 rebounds, a combination unparalleled in college history. His team won the national championship.

Randy Woods, *La Salle*
(1991–92)
Scored a national-best 847 points and had 160 assists, making him the only player to have the most points and assists during the same season in Big 5 history. Team won its fourth conference title in five years.

Tom Gola

Malik Rose, *Drexel*
(1995–96)
Averaged 20.2 points, 13.2 rebounds and shot 59.5 percent from the field. Team won its third consecutive conference title, finished 27–4 and got its school's only NCAA Tournament victory.

— Dick Jerardi

Big 5 Fixtures

Yo Yo: His real name was Harry Schifren. He used to sleep at the *Evening Bulletin.* Legend has it that he walked dogs for wealthy people in Rittenhouse Square. He passed away in 1979. But for two decades before that, he was a staple at Phillies games and at the Palestra, where he used to walk in for free. Coaches and players made a big fuss over him. Fans gave him quarters. He had carte blanche. He'd shoot free throws at halftime. He was the Big 5's unofficial mascot.

Jake Nevin: Villanova's lovable leprechaun. In title, he was the team's trainer. But he was so much more. In 1985, when the Wildcats won the NCAA championship, he was there in Lexington, Kentucky, in a wheelchair. He would pass away not long after that. They named the old gym in his

Jake Nevin

honor. When rumors had Rollie Massimino leaving to take a job with the Nets, Jake supposedly told him, "If I knew you'd leave, I wouldn't have let you win the title."

Bill Cosby: The most recognizable mascot this side of the Hawk.

— Mike Kern

Meet the Owl Without a Vowel

Bill Mlkvy, 71, had a dental practice in Yardley-Morrisville for 25 years until starting his own business in 1980. That business, Ultrasound Services Inc. (USI), has evolved into three more businesses with nearly 500 employees. He lives in Newtown (Bucks County) and every weekend (Thursday to Monday) is a long one at his house in Ocean City, New Jersey. Here he reflects on his Temple career:

Daily News: How did you score all those points (731 in 25 games) as a junior?

Mlkvy: The people I played with didn't perceive it (as me taking all the shots) . . . In those days, everything was centered around a player . . . What happened was they were coached around an individual. That individual handled the ball 50 percent of the time, so I'd bring up the ball. I had to learn all the positions. I played pivot. I played forward. I'd take a couple of shots from outside, a couple from the pivot, a couple on fastbreaks. The number would accumulate and that's how I scored my points. I always had the ball.

DN: What about the last game of that season when you scored 73 against Wilkes?

Mlkvy: It was another one of those perception things. We were just going up and down the court. I had a game where you make like five in a row and a couple of foul shots. All of a sudden, we were in the middle of the first half and I had like 22 points. The players got together and said let's give the ball to Bill. The whole thing evolved from midway through the first half until almost the end of the game. It was just a freak night. It was like a no-hitter. Something happens. Everything went right. The players were with me. The coach was with me. It just worked out.

DN: Why did your average drop to 17.4 points as a senior?

Mlkvy: I was in dental school. It wasn't called a graduate school. It was a professional school . . . The academics were just incredible. It just was overwhelming. And we had a new group of players. I was very fortunate to finish the year. I hardly went to practice.

DN: You were a territorial

Bill Mlkvy

draft choice of the Philadelphia Warriors, but your professional career lasted just one season. The Korean War intervened. You became a major in the Dental Corps and served in Korea.

Mlkvy: I had a five-year contract, but I could only play the one year. The fellows that I made the All-America team with, like Clyde Lovellette, all had long NBA careers. If I had been over 6-6, I would have been deferred [from Army service]. Clyde Lovellette played 15 years. That was one of the things that was a heartache to me. My senior year, going through that dental thing and then the one year of pro ball. I just never finished. It was like I never finished what I started out to do. I always wondered what level could I have reached. But then that kind of dissipated through the years. Life has been wonderful.

— Dick Jerardi

The Grand Finales

January 16, 1966
Seldom-used Steve Donches of nationally ranked St. Joseph's hits a 35-footer at the buzzer to beat Villanova at the Palestra, 71–69. The Holy War never had it so good.

December 26, 1962
Jimmy Boyle scores at the horn to give St. Joe's a 58–57 win over third-ranked Bowling Green at the Palestra in the first round of the Quaker City Tournament.

March 14, 1981
John Smith's layup at the buzzer gives St. Joe's a 49–48 win over top-ranked DePaul in the second round of the NCAA Tournament at Dayton, Ohio.

January 15, 1969
Sophomore Steve Bilsky hits a 25-footer as time expires to give Penn, which took the air out of the ball most of the way, a 32–30 upset of Villanova. A photo of it adorns the walls of the Palestra.

March 9, 2001
Lynn Greer converts all three free throws with 2.9 seconds remaining, rallying Temple to a 77–76 win over George Washington in the Atlantic 10 semifinals at the First Union Spectrum. The Owls seemingly had lost after trailing by 11 with 6 minutes left.

January 4, 1990
Loyola Marymount's Bo Kimble throws in a running 35-footer at the horn to beat host St. Joe's. He finishes with 54 points on 17-for-33 shooting, all Fieldhouse records.

The dotted line shows the flight of the Steve Bilsky game-winner vs. Villanova in 1969, giving Penn the upset win.

DAILY NEWS FILE PHOTO

I Remember

Off the top of my head . . . Lenny Wilkens, who played for Providence, stealing the ball in the last second to beat Villanova. I remember a Jack Ramsay team making it very difficult for Wilt to score. I remember Guy Rodgers going crazy in a playoff game, maybe the best game I've ever seen by someone in the backcourt. I can think of a hundred great things.

Maybe the one thing though, was the feeling of walking into the Palestra on a night when there was going to be a great Big 5 game. Just the anticipation . . . walking down those slanted ramps, going down to the locker room on a night when you were going to play St. Joe's or Villanova. It gave you goose-bumps. If you didn't get them with that, you weren't alive.

DICK HARTER
Boston Celtics assistant coach
Penn coach (1966–71)

March 15, 1984

Terence Stansbury hits a 35-footer at the buzzer to give Temple a 65–63 win over St. John's in Charlotte, North Carolina, in John Chaney's first NCAA Tournament game. It's the Owls' first NCAA win since 1958.

December 20, 1998

Pepe Sanchez makes two free throws with one second left to give sixth-ranked Temple a 60–59 win over No. 5 Michigan State at the Apollo. The Owls trail by double digits late in the second half. Sanchez falls backward onto the floor after swishing the game-winner and is engulfed by the storming crowd.

January 28, 1998

Sanchez swishes a heave from halfcourt to give the Owls a 70–67, double-overtime victory at McGonigle Hall over La Salle. But nobody gets to hear his side of the story, because John Chaney won't let his freshman talk.

February 6, 1990

After Paul Chambers misses a free throw with 1 second left, Hassan Duncombe muscles past Princeton's Kit Mueller and slams home a two-hander to give Penn a 51–50 victory at the Palestra. Says Princeton coach Pete Carril: "That is one of the more unacceptable ways to lose."

— Mike Kern

Best Visitors to Play Against Philly Teams

1. Oscar Robertson
Guard, University of Cincinnati
A first-team All-America player three times. He made two trips to Philadelphia during the 1958–59 season, when he averaged 32.6 points to lead the nation and 16.3 rebounds. Robertson and the Bearcats defeated St. Joseph's and Temple at the Palestra. The Big "O" was the first three-time Division I player of the year. In three seasons, Robertson totaled 2,973 points and 1,338 rebounds. When he was named the best player in 1959, he beat out Bailey Howell of Mississippi State and Jerry West of West Virginia.

2. Wilt Chamberlain
Center, Kansas University
The Philadelphia legend made his only trip home as a collegian on December 14, 1957. The Jayhawks defeated St. Joe's at the Palestra, 66–54. Chamberlain averaged 30.1 points during the 1957–58 season.

3. George Mikan
Center, DePaul University
The first great big man in the history of basketball was named to the All-America team three times before he went on to star in the NBA. Mikan helped DePaul defeat St. Joe's, 64–56, on December 28, 1943, at Convention Hall.

4. Jerry West

Guard, West Virginia University
The two-time All-America played his only game in Philly as a sophomore against Villanova at the Palestra. The Mountaineers edged the Wildcats, 76–75, on January 8, 1958. West averaged 17.8 points as a sophomore and went on to score 2,309 career points and have 1,240 rebounds in three seasons.

5. Bill Bradley

Forward, Princeton University
The best player in Ivy League history helped the Tigers beat Penn at the Palestra on March 4, 1964, and January 30, 1965. As a still mostly unknown sophomore, he was sensational in an 82–81 overtime loss to St. Joe's. The game was played March 11, 1963, at the Palestra. Bradley was a first-team All-America in each season. He was the 1965 player of the year, besting Rick Barry of Miami (Fla.), Cazzie Russell of Michigan and Gail Goodrich of UCLA.

Great Wall of Hoya: center Patrick Ewing

DAILY NEWS FILE PHOTO

6. Patrick Ewing

Center, Georgetown University
Three times a first-team All-America player, he made Big East Conference trips to play against Villanova from 1981 through 1985. He was the Naismith Award winner and the Associated Press player of the year in '85.

7. Wes Unseld

Center, Louisville University
The two-time first-team All-America played against La Salle on March 2, 1966, as a sophomore. During his junior year, Unseld and Louisville won the Quaker City Tournament at the Palestra, defeating Niagara, Syracuse and Princeton. Unseld is Louisville's all-time leading scorer as a three-year player with 1,686 points.

8. John Wooden

Guard, Purdue University
Before he became a Hall of Fame coach at UCLA, Wooden was the NCAA's first player to be named All-America three times, and was player of the year in 1932. The Wizard of West Lafayette helped Purdue beat Temple, 45–17, on January 1, 1931. Purdue went 42–8 in Wooden's three seasons.

9. Calvin Murphy
Guard, Niagara University
The greatest little man in NCAA history set a Palestra record by scoring 52 in a 100–83 victory over La Salle on December 16, 1967. He averaged 38.2 points in the 1967–68 season. Murphy, at 5-10, went on to become a two-time first-team All-America.

10. Adrian Dantley
Forward, Notre Dame University
Twice named a first-team All-America, he played a game in Philly in each of his three seasons: on February 6, 1974, in a 98–78 victory against La Salle; on January 11, 1975, against Villanova, in a 125–90 victory at the Palestra; and on February 4, 1976, in a 108–89 victory over La Salle at the Spectrum. Dantley averaged 25.8 points and 9.8 rebounds in his career.

11. Ralph Sampson
Center, Virginia
Came into town as a freshman on December 5, 1979, when he had 12 points, 13 rebounds and nine blocks in a 58–52 victory over Temple. His next visit took place in 1981, when the Final Four was held at the Spectrum. In a 78–65 loss to North Carolina on March 28, he scored 11 on 3-for-10 shooting. Two days later, he scored 10 and fouled out in the third-place game, a 78–74 victory over Louisiana State.

12. David Robinson
Center, Navy
A two-time All-America during his four-year career, Robinson had a memorable game against Drexel in a January 21, 1987, visit to the Palestra. He had 44 points, 14 rebounds and two blocked shots, but the Dragons (7–7) pulled off an 83–80 upset win over the 18th-ranked Middies (12–4).

13. Chris Mullin
Guard/forward, St. John's
The most honored player in school history made four trips during his distinguished career to play Big East rival Villanova. As a freshman, on January 11, 1982, he was held to 11 in a 64–62 loss at the Field House. In a classic at the Spectrum on February 26, 1983, he scored 25, but his miss at the free-throw line set up John Pinone's 17-footer that gave Villanova a 71–70 overtime win. Mullin scored 25 on March 3, 1984, when Villanova once again won in overtime, 73–72, at the Palestra. He got his revenge as a senior on February 9, 1985, scoring 17 straight points in a 70–68 victory at the Spectrum.

— John Smallwood

Whetting Appetites Off the Court

Here's a list of places where the "in" crowd has hung out before or after games through the years.

Cavanaugh's
(Market Street)

If you left the Palestra via the back door, waded through the exiting cars up the driveway that passed for 32nd Street, under the Walnut Street bridge and onto Chestnut Street, you were within a heartbeat of Cavanaugh's back door.

There, most of the 9,000 or so with whom you had just enjoyed the game would hash and rehash not just that night's contest but every team, every player, every play ever acted out in the Big House.

It had a midwinter ambience even in July.

Cavanaugh's
(City Avenue)

The real decision after every St. Joseph's home game was not where to go, but whether to cross City Avenue at the light or not.

If you decided on the diagonal route, you had a better shot at a seat, if you were lucky enough to avoid needing a bed at Lankenau Hospital.

Frieda's

Never heard of it? The food truck at the entrance to the Palestra parking lot (yes, there is a Palestra parking lot, although *lot* might not be the correct term) was there for daytime Palestra and Franklin Field employees,

Cavanaugh's

and no doubt served a pregame meal or a thousand for game officials, reporters, fans and probably even a recruit or two.

That's not to be confused with the guy a few more feet up 33rd Street, selling pretzels and pennants as you made your way up the Palestra pavement on the north side of the tennis courts.

New Deck

Snuggled into the middle of Sansom Street a few blocks from the Palestra, it serves as a convenient neutral site for factions of two campuses.

> ### I Remember
>
> The passion, on and off the court, especially when I was playing the Celtics. That was such a high for people. You could have been playing bad for most of the season, but you'd get ready to play the Celtics and people on the street would tell you, "You can't lose this game." You'd get in the arena, there was a different feeling, a different air, that passion that the people in Philadelphia have for basketball, period. I have never seen it like that anywhere else.
>
> *MAURICE CHEEKS*
> *Portland Trail Blazers head coach, former Sixers guard*

It is so neutral, in fact, that we think the men's room is actually on Drexel's campus and the women's room is on Penn's.

— *Bob Vetrone Jr.*

The Palestra

Two custodians maintain the arena's "living museum," where the dead still stop in to play

Dan Harrell understands the Palestra, now in its 76th year. "It's like knowing somebody," he says. "It is like a person."

To understand a person, you need to know what's inside. Harrell, the Palestra's custodian for the last decade, knows. So does Tony Crosson, who describes himself as the Palestra's "conductor of electricity." He's been in the place for 42 years. "And I was sneaking into games for 15 years before that."

Harrell and Crosson know every inch of the Palestra's catacombs. They walk easily through the two sets of tunnels just beyond the court. They know when walls went up and when they came down. And yes, the building does have ghosts.

"Believe me when I tell you that there are spirits," Harrell says. "You can call me crazy, but I know they are here. If there are ghosts, they are pretty good guys. You see them and then they're gone. Come in by yourself and you'll see."

There is nothing, Harrell says, like being in the Palestra on a summer day at 5 a.m.

"The building," he says, "is happy with itself then."

The Palestra was built in 1927.

DAILY NEWS FILE PHOTO

He likes to sit in his office with his Wawa coffee and the morning paper. Then, he does the cryptogram and "listens to the ghosts play basketball."

Tour the inner sanctum of the Palestra with Tony and Dan, you get history and comedy. You find out that the old floor was laid horizontally, prompting visitors to become disoriented. Some of the old floor remains under the stands and beyond the walls. The newer, vertical floor is around 25 years old. An old picture beyond the walls reveals that there were once row houses where the tennis courts in front of the building are now.

Every nook and every cranny has a story. Dan tells the one about the street person he discovered inside a very tiny locker one day before a game. Dan heard something and thought it was Tony playing a joke on him. Then he opened the locker and the man bolted out of the locker, ran through one of the tunnels and under the east stands right toward Tony.

"Tony wasn't fast enough to catch him," Dan says.

Tony did not want to catch him, Tony says.

Probably came in through "Hutch," otherwise known as Hutchinson Gym, the annex to the Palestra. Tony and Dan open a few doors, walk through some tunnels and down a very old set of wooden steps ("I know they were here 60 years ago and looking just like this," Tony says) into a vast room that they say is under Hutch.

"If you got into Hutchinson Gym, you got into the Palestra," Tony says.

They show how. Back up the old stairs, down a few tunnels and through a door that now leads to the women's basketball locker room under the west stands. In those days, the door led right under the stands. There was a guard who understood what was up with all the people coming through that door. He wasn't too concerned about it.

"I don't know what you're doing here, but I think there's a seat over there," Dan quotes the guard as saying.

"[Fran] Dunphy used to sneak in through the windows," Tony says of Penn's basketball coach. "Dunphy never bought a ticket."

Now, he doesn't have to.

"I grew up in Southwest Philly, same neighborhood as Dunphy," Harrell says. "He just doesn't admit it."

Wind blows through the tunnels. Because of changes in the building through the years, air is often looking for a place to go, causing doors to slam without apparent provocation. It could be the ghosts.

Those old pictures that used to hang in the Palestra displays before the makeover in 2000? Many are now in the catacombs gathering dust, along with what has to be the original backboards, the ones that hung from cables. Remember?

Old trophy cases and the original turnstiles are still around while somebody figures out what to do with them.

"We've got a lot of old stuff," Tony says. "We don't even know what some of it is."

Somebody did not like former president Richard Nixon. His name is all over the inside walls. He was not praised.

Anyone wanting a history lesson in Philadelphia basketball should walk the corridor that rings the Palestra.

ALEJANDRO A. ALVAREZ / DAILY NEWS

The wiring does not appear to be state of the art.

"It's probably illegal," Tony says. "Doesn't matter here."

There's a giant, old safe that belonged to Ogden, the concessionaires. The owner died and, according to Tony, "they never found the combination."

"Could be a lot of money in it," Tony says.

Each locker room has its own story. When Lower Merion and Kobe Bryant won the District 1 championship and earned a trip to Hershey in 1996, the team celebrated by tossing Hershey's Kisses around the locker room. They were crushed into the red carpet.

"I should get that bill and send it to Kobe," Harrell says. "He can afford it."

Harrell never liked that red carpet anyway.

"It looks like a South Philly go-go joint," he says.

Wrestlers, Dan says, are the worst.

"They like to throw things when they lose," he says. "It takes an extra two days to clean up after wrestling."

Dan points out that the Palestra must have the last scoreboard where you have to go up and change the names of the teams by hand.

Just inside the women's locker room is a set of four light switches. One night not long after he started, Dan decided he should turn those lights out during a Penn-Columbia game.

"Do they look like the place where normal switches would be?" Tony asks.

No, actually, they don't. In fact, they are not normal light switches. They control the lights over the Palestra court. Dan turned them off and the building went dark while a Columbia player was attempting a jump shot.

"He walked out like he had nothing to do with it," Tony says.

"The only thing on was the scoreboard," Dan says. "It was pitch black. I snuck out and crawled under the stands."

There was the night they gave out stickers that ended up all over, sticking to everything.

"Mustard packets are the worst," Dan says. "You step on them and they squirt all over the place."

"There's millions of stories here," Tony says.

They would know. They have been there for most of them.

—Dick Jerardi

A museum in its own right, the Palestra forms the backdrop for "curators" Dan Harrell (left) and Tony Crosson.

ALEJANDRO A. ALVAREZ / DAILY NEWS

Voice of the Big 5

Dan Baker can still remember the first college basketball game he called on the radio: Alabama vs. La Salle, at the Palestra, on December 4, 1977.

He's done almost 1,100 more since then. Along the way, he probably has had nearly that many on-air partners.

"At the time, I never thought it would amount to this," Baker said. "It's been some ride."

That ride was recognized on February 18, 2002, at halftime of Drexel's home game against North Carolina–Wilmington, when Baker was honored for his 25th anniversary in the business.

Then, of course, he went back to the sideline and called the final 20 minutes.

"At first, I did it to supplement my income," he said. "Over the years, it just grew."

Baker, the PA voice for the Phillies for the last three decades, began broadcasting Drexel games during the 1997–98 season. He's done play-by-play for all six Division I schools in the city. The highlight? Going to the Final Four with Penn in 1979.

Baker, who taught sixth graders in the public system for 12 years, also called some 100 Temple football games. And he was the Big 5's executive director from 1981 to '96.

Quite a résumé. But the thing he's most proud of is the fact that many of the people he's worked with were there to help him celebrate this moment. It's quite a roll call, from Bill Campbell to Bob Vetrone to Pat Delsi to Scott Graham.

"The funny thing is, I helped a lot of those guys break into the business," Baker said. "And a lot of them helped me. When I look back, it's very gratifying."

At the now closed Landreth Elementary School, 23rd and Federal Streets, Baker once taught a young Gene Banks.

"While he was agile and tall for his age, I had no idea he'd turn out to be such a great player," he recalled. "We had a few other kids who were better but just never developed. Shows you what I know."

— *Mike Kern*

I Remember

The Palestra, what else? I'll never forget being a young kid and playing on that court for the first time. It was exhilarating, like a dream coming true. I was a skinny sophomore on the JV at West and the varsity was in the Catholic League playoffs at the Palestra. I was thrilled when I was told I'd be dressing with the varsity and sitting on the bench at the Palestra. And then, I actually got in the game! I missed a free throw. But I remember, when I went in, I had the chills. Jim Boyle, a JV kid, getting in a varsity playoff game at the Palestra. It was out of this world. I was doing what every kid in Philly dreamed of, playing at the Palestra.

JIM BOYLE
West Catholic, St. Joe's, Big 5 Hall of Fame

A Baker's Dozen of Most Memorable Broadcasts

(in chronological order)

March 11, 1979

At Reynolds Coliseum in Raleigh, North Carolina. Penn 72, No. 2 UNC 71. Second round of NCAA Tournament. That year, Penn went to the Final Four. What stands out? "The stunned crowd. It was a twin killing that day. St. John's beat Duke in the other game that day."

February 28, 1981

At the Palestra. Villanova 72, St. Joseph's 62. It was the last Big 5 game of the season, Rollie Massimino coaching against Jimmy Lynam. A sellout crowd. What stands out? "What made it unique is that it was the only time that the Big 5, in its full round-robin format, finished in a five-way tie."

February 7, 1984

At the Palestra. St. Joe's 58, No. 2 DePaul 45. A near sellout. DePaul was 17–0 coming in, coached by Ray Meyer. Jim Boyle was St. Joe's coach. What stands out? "The crowd swarming the floor."

Temple's Tim Perry and Villanova's Mark Plansky duel beneath the basket.

DAILY NEWS FILE PHOTO

January 14, 1988

At McGonigle Hall. Temple 59, La Salle 56. Sellout crowd. John Chaney's best team, No. 1 most of the season. La Salle finished 24–10 but 0–4 in the Big 5. What stands out? "Just the way Temple prevailed. John Chaney always seems to find a way to win."

January 4, 1990

At Alumni Memorial Fieldhouse. Loyola Marymount 99, St. Joe's 96. Marked the return of prodigal sons Bo Kimble and Hank Gathers. Kimble won the game with a buzzer-beater and scored 54, breaking Oscar Robertson's record of most points vs. St. Joe's. What stands out? "It was end to end, racehorse basketball. [At the finish], Kimble barely made it into the frontcourt and unleashed a bomb from the left sideline. It was just incredible."

February 6, 1990

At the Palestra. Penn 51, Princeton 50. One of the great Penn-Princeton games, not one of the great Penn teams. One second left. Paul Chambers, one of the best playmakers in Penn history, goes to the line to shoot one-and-one. What stands out? "He missed the front end, and then Hassan Duncombe jumped up and all of a sudden tipped in the missed shot."

February 22, 1990

At the Civic Center. La Salle 100, Manhattan 60. Steve Lappas was Manhattan's coach. Lionel Simmons became the fifth player in NCAA history to score 3,000 points or more. What stands out? "La Salle had blue and gold balloons in a big net at the top of the Civic Center. When he scored [his 3,000th] on a free throw, they pulled the net, releasing thousands of blue and gold balloons."

February 16, 1991

At the Civic Center. St. Joe's 82, La Salle 73. Before a sellout crowd, St. Joe's won to claim a share of the Big 5 title. It was the last City Series game played in the full round-robin format. What stands out? "There were coaches in the Big 5 saying that the City Series games were insignificant, that fans didn't care as much. St. Joe's had a losing record, but the game meant everything to them. They played their hearts out."

December 9, 1991

At the Spectrum. La Salle 79, Villanova 75. It was in the first year of the new City Series format. What stands out? "The school many people blamed for the change was Villanova, so when they came to the floor, they were booed unmercifully. The atmosphere was unbelievable. It was a great game played by two great teams."

March 9, 1992

At Knickerbocker Arena in Albany, New York. La Salle 77, Manhattan 76. Championship game of Metro Atlantic Athletic Conference. Speedy Morris vs. Steve Lappas. Bron Holland hit a jumper with 11 seconds left to win the game, sending La Salle to the NCAAs. What stands out? "The wild celebration at the Hilton Hotel in Albany."

March 17, 1994

At the Nassau Coliseum. Penn 90, Nebraska 80. First round of NCAA Tournament. Barry Pierce scored 25. What stands out? "There were always questions like, 'Can the Ivy champ be competitive in the NCAAs?' Penn looked very good."

March 16, 1996

At the Baltimore Arena. NCAA Tournament game. Alabama 91, Penn 85. Jerome Allen had 30 in a losing cause. What stands out? "My son Darren kept the stats. It was one of the first games he did that. That was a doubleheader game. Drexel, with Malik Rose, played in the other game."

March 15, 1997

At the University of Utah. St. Joe's 81, Boston College 77, in overtime. It was the same site where Penn played in the Final Four. What stands out? "Rasheed Bey, who was brilliant that year, scored 10 of St. Joe's 12 points in overtime, and 23 overall, and eight assists. That allowed them to advance to the Western Regional finals."

A View from the Outside

"Best Place for College Basketball . . . Has Always Been Philadelphia"

I grew up in New York City, going to the old eight-team Holiday Festival and the NIT back when the entire tournament was played in Madison Square Garden. I have lived my entire adult life in Washington, D.C., spending countless hours in Cole Field House, watching Georgetown rise to power and remembering the good old days when American University played in Fort Myer, Virginia, where the teams used the weight rooms as locker rooms.

But the best place for college basketball, in my mind, has always been Philadelphia, and the place in Philadelphia will always be the Palestra. There is nothing quite like the Big 5, even if selfishness and greed almost killed it during the 1980s. The notion of taking Big 5 games out of the Palestra and putting them at on-campus sites was the worst idea ever this side of New Coke. Choosing not to play in the Palestra is a little bit like having the chance to eat at Bookbinder's (they closed The Original, are you kidding me?) and opting for Red Lobster.

To wallow in the seedy politics that moved the games out of the Palestra and, for a while, cut the number of Big 5 games played each year in half, is pointless. At least nowadays, there is an effort being made to get things back to where they should be.

Philadelphia hoops has had so many great moments, so many great players and coaches and has so much tradition that picking one thing out as standing above the rest is almost impossible. But for me, Villanova's improbable run to the 1985 NCAA title stands out because I had the chance to be there for all six games and to get a close-up look at that joyride, courtesy of my unique friendship with Rollie Massimino.

I am certain that I wasn't the first person to call him the Danny DeVito of college basketball, I'm just not that clever, but when I used the phrase in the *Washington Post* prior to a Villanova-Maryland game that season, Rollie called me out on it. "You know how much this suit costs?" he screamed at me. "It costs more than your entire wardrobe is worth."

He had me there.

I went looking for help and found it in Rollie's son, R.C., who was a walk-on guard on that team. "Oh sure," R.C. said, "he starts out the game looking like a million bucks. But then, as it goes on he just . . . unravels."

Bless you, R.C. I couldn't get the quote in the paper fast enough. The next time I encountered Rollie was in Dayton, where Villanova was sent to open the NCAA Tournament as a No. 8 seed in the Southeast

Regional, getting to play the host team on its home court in the first round. "Turning my own son on me," he said, trying not to laugh. "You straps are all the same."

Do not go to your dictionary to look up "straps." It is short for "strap-hangers," which is Rollie's term of endearment for those of us from New York. He called me a few other endearing names, none of which can be printed.

A friendship bloomed.

Villanova beat Dayton by one and then shocked top-seeded Michigan in the second round. I spent a large chunk of the next week in Philly, since Villanova was now playing Maryland in the Sweet 16. Rollie was in his glory, threatening to ban me from practice since I was a "spy" for Lefty Driesell. Lefty got a hoot out of that. We all know what happened after that: Villanova beat Maryland and North Carolina in Birmingham, Alabama, and Rollie was all over "you ACC guys" in the aftermath. Then came the Miracle of Lexington, still the most remarkable performance in a final I've ever witnessed.

When it was over, Rollie said to me, "So you want to fly back with us for the celebration?"

Damn right, I did. The plane left at 7 in the morning and when it landed, we were all loaded on open flatbeds for the trip downtown. It looked like the whole city had come out to celebrate. And when the team got to City Hall, Rollie stood up in front of the cheering masses and started to give a victory speech. He was doing just fine until he got to "And then we went and won the national championship." His voice cracked on the last two words as if it had just hit him what he and his kids had accomplished.

I stood there, the strap-hanger, ACC guy, thinking to myself, there's just no place like Philly for college hoops.

All these years later, that is still the case.

— *John Feinstein*
The Washington Post

Chapter Four

The Women

Once Again, Philly's Leading the Rush   SAM DONNELLON

The Web sites are countless. So are the number of teams and towns involved in women's and girls' basketball.

Division I college programs now demand a full-time commitment from their scholarship athletes, some hoping that a surge toward the elite will result in increased visibility for the school and increased contributions to the school.

"It's crazy now," says Cathy Rush, who, as Immaculata's coach during their three championships in the early 1970s, was there at the infancy of the insanity.

The Amateur Athletic Union (AAU), which oversees elite travel teams throughout the land, reported 120,000 girls enrolled nationwide in 2001, up exponentially from the 18,675 enrolled just a decade ago. In the Philadelphia area, participation in AAU basketball increased from 374 girls in 1992 to 3,571 in 2001.

"It's become socially acceptable for girls to sweat," said Eddie Clinton, AAU senior sports manager in charge of women's basketball.

Profitable, too. Today in women's and girls' basketball, there are sponsor-driven championships and sneaker contracts and a professional league that, this time, seems built to last.

Women's basketball even has bona fide and recognizable stars these days. In the college game, perennial powers like Connecticut and Tennessee make household names of their top players, and elite pro stars endorse sneakers and basketballs.

"There used to be a saying," Cathy Rush mused recently. "Animals sweat. Men perspire. Women glow."

No more. Whether it is college, high school or in youth leagues around the area, girls sweat, perspire and, if they are good enough, glow.

Scholarships are at stake. State championships, too.

Ten thousand girls, most from the Philadelphia area, arrive at The Future Stars Camp at Swarthmore College every summer in a quest to become better, some maybe with a dream to play for Illinois' Theresa Grentz or Rutgers' Vivian Stringer or Connecticut's Geno Auriemma, or any of those other big-time college coaches they have read or heard about.

Ten thousand girls come and hear Cathy Rush tell those tried-and-true stories not just of Immaculata College, but of the Catholic League games that set the table for those championships and established basketball as a socially acceptable avocation of girls in Philadelphia.

That's up from the 45 kids who attended Rush's first camp in 1970, before Title IX, and before Immaculata charmed this town, and the nation, too, with the first of its improbable run of three AIAW titles (the AIAW preceded the NCAA as the governing organization of women's athletics). Ninety kids followed in 1971, and once the publicized story of a small all-girls college became a national phenomenon, Rush's camp increased by 600 in 1972, by 1,200 in 1973 and increased each year to its current capacity level.

> ## I Remember
>
> Greetings from Osaka, Japan. It is a long way from the outdoor courts at Shaw Jr. High — 54th and Warrington Avenue — where I first played hoops. Random memories of Philadelphia basketball: 1970, La Salle–Villanova, Durrett vs. Porter, only no Durrett, on the bench with a knee injury and crying like a small boy. The Explorers do the impossible and win. That game is Big 5 — Philly ball. Nowhere in my travels was the game played with more meaning. It was our life, the players knew it, the fans knew it, the city knew it. Since then I have had some great moments in basketball, but that one game was enough for a lifetime. Sayonara.
>
> *PAUL WESTHEAD*
> *Coach, pro team in Osaka, Japan*
> *La Salle coach (1970–79)*

"As a dad, you're glad your daughter is playing sports," Rush said. "That was not necessarily true 20 years ago."

Title IX was the vehicle that changed all that. But Immaculata's run was the model. Mighty Mac players washed their own uniforms, raised money for trips and went to college for many reasons, none of them basketball.

"There was no better team," Rush said, "to jump-start women's college basketball."

Some hadn't even played on an organized team until they arrived at the school. But the nucleus who did consisted of Catholic League players.

And the games back then, between Archbishop Prendergast, Little Flower and St. Hubert, among others, were just as spirited, just as well attended as they are today, Rush said.

They would annually bus fans into the Palestra during their playoffs, attracting as many as 8,000 people for their pre–Title IX games. "They would still be in school uniforms," Rush said. "So you would see pockets of different colors circling the Palestra."

The more things change, the more they remain the same. Rush was in a rush, heading out to a much-anticipated tilt between Cardinal O'Hara and Archbishop Carroll.

Tickets were hard to come by, and she wanted to get there early.

Back in Orlando, Florida, where AAU headquarters is located, Clinton was talking about his memories of Immaculata, and the jump-start it gave girls' basketball nationwide.

"It's been so long ago now," he said wistfully, "that most of the kids playing now don't know about it."

— *Sam Donnellon*

The Mighty Mighty Macs

A basketball dynasty that shook up the country

Special times in sports are to savor. Immaculata College's reign in women's basketball was one of those special times for Philadelphia fans.

Back in the 1970s, before women's basketball was discovered by network television, Immaculata's "Mighty Macs" were the women's hoops story.

The then 500-student Catholic college in Frazer, Pennsylvania, won three consecutive national championships (1972–74).

Backed by their bucket-clanging fans, including nuns, the Macs played in Madison Square Garden, and at North Carolina State, Kansas and Nevada–Las Vegas. Colleges across the nation paid Immaculata's expenses to bring the magical Macs to their arenas.

Immaculata's center, Theresa Shank, was a three-time player of the year.

The Macs' coach, Cathy Rush, is in the Women's Basketball Hall of Fame.

Among the Macs who developed into prominent coaches are Rene Muth Portland at Penn State and Theresa Shank, now Theresa Grentz, at Illinois. Marianne Stanley coached at Old Dominion, Pennsylvania, Southern California and California, and in the WNBA. Mary Scharff later coached Immaculata.

It's stunning to remember that the Macs weren't recruited to build a championship team.

On the 20th anniversary of the Macs' first championship, Denise Conway Crawford, who played on all three title teams, told the *Daily News*: "Not one of us went there to play basketball. There were no sports scholarships. Of that original team, five of the players were from Archbishop Prendergast, and I was the only one of those five who even played high school ball."

Rush said: "Everybody went there for an education. Everybody was biology and pre-med and pre-law. It was an amazing group of young women, before being a young woman athlete was really cool."

Coach Cathy Rush (far left) and the Mighty Macs return home from Manhattan, Kansas, after beating Mississippi College for their third straight AIAW title in March 1974.

ROBERT HALVEY COLLECTION

Immaculata's team was so underfunded that the players had to sell toothbrushes to finance their first trip to the AIAW Tournament. Players washed their own uniforms in hotel sinks.

Watching a Connecticut victory at Tennessee with 25,000 fans in the Thompson-Boling Arena in Knoxville brought back fond memories of Immaculata for Rush.

"Immaculata did not have a home court my first year," she said. "My second year, a gym was built. It was a physical education facility and didn't have bleachers.

"The year after we won the national championship, beating West Chester, the following year we played West Chester at a typical women's college game time: 3 o'clock on a Monday afternoon. No one knew anything about it. When we arrived at West Chester, it was a standing-room-only crowd [admission was free].

"I looked around and said, 'Wow! Things are happening.'"

Immaculata rented the Jake Nevin Field House at Villanova. The Macs played at Cardinal O'Hara and Ridley high schools.

"We might have been one of the first [women's] teams to charge admission, and people actually paid [to attend]," Rush said. "I went to a committee of [Immaculata] nuns and said, 'I think we can make some money doing this.'

"We had to pay $100 to rent the gyms. One nun said, 'What if no one comes?' I was being paid $500 a year. I said, 'Sister, I'll pay the $100 if I can't get the gate.' She said, 'We'll pay the $100.' I think 3,000 people came, at $2 apiece."

I Remember

One had to do with the fans. This guy for years had courtside seats, and he'd always have two different young ladies with him at the game. And he was one of those guys who would select a player for that year, and he would get on that guy unmercifully. I happened to be his target one season. He would start during warmups and never let up until the end of the ballgame. One night, at the tail end of the season, he was on my case. Now, he would stand up, he was more on the chunky side, and he started pointing a finger at me, yelling at me, and I happened to glance over there, and his fly was open. So in a stage whisper that you could hear in the last row in the balcony . . . I [shout at him that] "it's OK for you to yell at me, but I'm not going to listen to you when your fly is open." Everyone in the building started laughing. That guy never came back again.

TOMMY HEINSOHN
Boston Celtics (1956–65)

Thanks in large part to the Mighty Macs, women's basketball advanced rapidly.

"We all thought it would happen," Rush said. "I don't think anyone thought it would happen this soon. When Carol Eckman started coaching at West Chester and I just started at Immaculata, the game had just gone from the old six-player game to the five-player game. People weren't sure the girls could keep up. They'd say, 'You know, it's a lot of running.'"

The Macs ran and shot their way into the hearts of Philadelphia's rich basketball tradition.

— Bill Fleischman

Best of the Best

Linda Page, Murrell Dobbins Tech, 100 points vs. Jules Mastbaum Tech, February 13, 1981. Page, a 5-11 guard, hit the century mark with 48 seconds remaining on two free throws. Her total broke Wilt Chamberlain's city scoring record of 90 points vs. Roxborough, set in 1955. She was the most coveted schoolgirl player in the country in 1981, and went on to attend North Carolina State.

Linda Page

DAILY NEWS FILE PHOTO

Greatest College Single-Game Performances

Shelly Pennefather, *Villanova*
44 points vs. Cheyney, 1985; Villanova won, 109–60.

Dale Hodges, *St. Joseph's*
42 points vs. Temple, 1990; St. Joe's won, 77–62.

Marilyn Stephens, *Temple*
41 points vs. George Mason, 1983; Temple won, 91–56.

Dale Hodges
34 points and 19 rebounds vs. Penn State, 1990; St. Joe's won, 73–61.

Kristin Brendel, *Penn*
37 points and 21 rebounds vs. Harvard, 1991; Harvard won, 98–90.

Five Best Games

Immaculata 53, West Chester 48
(1972)
Championship game of the first AIAW tournament . . . Mighty Macs (24–1) avenged their only defeat of the season, 70–38, to West Chester in the AIAW Regional final.

St. Joseph's 61, Iowa 60
(1984)
Jim Foster, now at Ohio State, matched coaching strategy with former Cheyney coach Vivian Stringer, now at Rutgers.

La Salle 72, Connecticut 63
(1989)
NCAA Tournament game. UConn (24–5) had won the Big East Tournament.

Villanova 63, St. Joseph's 61, OT
(1989)
First televised Big 5 game.

Villanova 59, Rutgers 55
(1982)
Eastern championship of the AIAW.

— Bill Fleischman

Best of Philly's Females

(in alphabetical order)

Debbie Black, *St. Joseph's*
(1985–88)

Known as best all-around female athlete in school history . . . fiery point guard who led the Hawks to four consecutive NCAA Tournaments . . . school career leader in steals and second in assists . . . a WNBA All-Star.

Diana Caramanico, *Pennsylvania*
(1998–2001)

Quakers' all-time leading female scorer with 1,808 points . . . three-time Ivy League Player of the Year . . . as a senior, led the Quakers to first Ivy League title and NCAA Tournament appearance . . . No. 2 in the nation in rebounding (12.8) and seventh in scoring (22.7) as a senior.

Jennifer Cole, *La Salle*
(1989–93)

Explorers' all-time leading scorer with 1,875 points . . . at La Salle, first women's basketball player to have her number retired . . . Big 5 Player of the Year . . . MVP of the Metro Atlantic Athletic Conference.

Dale Hodges, *St. Joseph's*
(1988–90)

Acknowledged as greatest player in school history . . . scored 2,077 points and collected 1,049 rebounds . . . holds more than 30 school records, including rebounds and blocked shots (96) . . . scored career-high 42 points vs. Temple in 77–62 victory in 1990 . . . later played pro ball overseas.

In 2000–01, Penn's Diana Caramanico was among the nation's leaders in rebounding (second) and scoring (seventh).

GEORGE REYNOLDS / DAILY NEWS

Yolanda Laney, *Cheyney*
(1980–84)

Her 2,173 points are tied for second in Pennsylvania State Athletic Conference history . . . her 739 points during the 1983–84 season are a conference and school record.

Susan Moran, *St. Joseph's*
(1998–2002)

On February 8, 2002, scored 24 to pass Hodges and become the Hawks' all-time leading scorer in school history . . . finished fifth in scoring nationally in the 2000–01 season, averaging 22.6.

Shelly Pennefather, *Villanova*
(1983–87)
All-time leading scorer among Philly-area female players with 2,408 points (20.5 average) . . . top performance: 44 points vs. Cheyney in December 1985 . . . three-time Big East Conference Player of the Year . . . three-time Big 5 Player of the Year . . . also Wildcats' all-time rebounder (1,171, 10.0 average).

I Remember

Villanova beating Georgetown for the national championship. The night of the game was the opening night of the Garden State Racetrack. I went with a bunch of friends and the game was on, but with no volume. So we watched it without the crowd noise, without knowing they were making 70 percent of their shots.

[Philadelphia basketball, you think] point guards. All the great ones that have come out of here. Those great Penn teams, holding the ball, winning with great ballhandling skills and playing smart rather than relying on just athleticism.

CATHY RUSH
Former coach, Immaculata College

Theresa Shank, *Immaculata*
(1971–74)
Helped the Macs win three national championships . . . finished career with 1,167 points and 1,027 rebounds . . . three-time first-team All-America . . . 1974 player of the year.

Dawn Staley, *Virginia*
(1989–92)
A three-time All-America who helped the Cavaliers earn spots in four NCAA Tournaments, including three Final Fours . . . a product of Murrell Dobbins Tech in Philadelphia . . . starred on two gold medal–winning Olympic teams . . . WNBA veteran . . . Temple's women's coach.

Marianne Stanley, *Immaculata*
(1973–76)
Two-time All-America who was one of the country's first elite point guards . . . finished career with 544 assists . . . later coached at Old Dominion, Pennsylvania, USC and California, and in the WNBA.

Marilyn Stephens, *Temple*
(1980–84)
Scored 2,194 points, making her Temple's all-time leading female scorer . . . also team's all-time leading rebounder, with 1,516 . . . scored 41 points vs. George Mason in 1983 . . . first-team All-America in 1984.

Valerie Walker, *Cheyney*
(1978–82)
Scored 2,289 points, tops in Pennsylvania State Athletic Conference history . . . first-team All-America.

Honorable mention:
Theresa Carmichael, St. Joseph's; Chrissie Donahue, La Salle; Nancy Bernhardt and Lisa Ortlip, Villanova; Kristin Brendel, Pennsylvania; June Olkowski, Patty and Mary Coyle, Rutgers; Kristen Clement, Tennessee.

— *Bill Fleischman*

Vivian Stringer

ALLSPORT

Top Five Coaches (of Philly teams)

(in alphabetical order)
Jim Foster, St. Joe's
Stephanie V. Gaitley, St. Joe's
John Miller, La Salle
Harry Perretta, Villanova
Cathy Rush, Immaculata

Top Five Coaches (with Philly roots)

(in alphabetical order)
Geno Auriemma, Connecticut
Theresa Grentz, Illinois
Joe McKeown, George Washington
Rene Portland, Penn State
Vivian Stringer, Rutgers

— Bill Fleischman

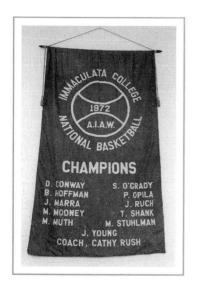

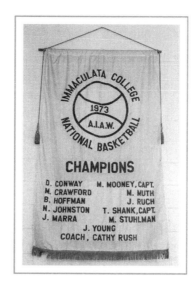

A View from the Outside

"Elvis/Bob Schafer. Doesn't everyone make that connection?"

Philly memories? Pull up a chair.

Outside the 215 area code, I can usually pull rank. I say things like, "Yeah, well, were you there when Villanova beat Rio Grande and Bevo Francis by a point at the Arena? I was." That tends to shut them up. Or I'll say, "Look, pal, I didn't see you at the Furman–La Salle game (Selvy vs. Gola, in other words) back in '53." That one gets the job done, too.

Hey, look. I'm no Bob Vetrone or Hoops Weiss. I'm no Herm Rogul or Harvey Pollack. But I can usually hold my own when the subject turns to Philly basketball. People like Hoops and Phil Jasner know I am the lifetime chairman of the Maurice Cheeks Fan Club. I'm always telling people that the 9–73 Sixer team was a better club than they think. And I'm on record as saying that Andrew Toney is the greatest forgotten player in NBA history.

I grew up in Trenton. My first connection to Philly basketball came when my father became the assistant athletic director at Villanova in 1952. Over the next two winters my father, mother and I spent every Friday and/or Saturday night attending a doubleheader at either the Palestra (home of Villanova, as well as Penn) or Convention Hall (where St. Joe's, Temple and La Salle were the regulars). So we're talking official pre–Big 5. The names were Tom Gola, Charley Singley, Ernie Beck, Larry Hennessy, Bob Schafer, Jack Devine and, of course, the Owl Without a Vowel (Bill Mlkvy), later followed by Hal (King) Lear and the great Guy Rodgers. To this day I have no trouble remembering that January 8 is Elvis Presley's birthday, because January 8, 1954, was the date when Schafer broke Hennessy's Palestra scoring record of 45 with 46 against Baldwin-Wallace. Elvis/Bob Schafer. Doesn't everyone make that connection?

I matured into a classic Big 5 fanatic. La Salle won it all in 1954 (a year before the Big 5 was formed) and Temple went to the Final Four in 1956 and '58. I loved Villanova most of all, of course, and thus had a love/hate relationship with St. Joe's. But let the record show I rooted for them in 1961 and was troubled by the bad news [a national point-shaving scandal that affected St. Joe's, among others] when it came. By the time I was 14 I thought that Les Keiter had the greatest job in the known universe. I couldn't imagine a better life than broadcasting all those Big 5 games.

Oh, and how about those Warriors? To me, Philly was the center of the basketball world, and was that ever more true than in 1956, when the Warriors won the NBA title with a roster that included six players who had come from Philly schools?

Philly basketball in the '60s meant epic Villanova–St. Joe's games (conveniently scheduled on or near my birthday) and even more epic Philadelphia-Celtics NBA collisions. And that brings me to The Zink.

There never was and never will be anything remotely like Dave Zinkoff. Who can possibly think of Philadelphia basketball without hearing in your head "Two minutes, twooooooooooo minutes left to go in this ballgame"? Or "And that is the quota on (fill in the blank)," or even "Have you got your program?" In the long run, The Zink was bad for basketball because he spawned so many pathetic and annoying imitators. But, oh, what I wouldn't give for The Zink to come back to handle the mike for a Sixers playoff game.

Memories . . . Being present when St. Joseph's Jimmy Boyle's jumper knocked off undefeated Bowling Green (Nate Thurmond, Howie Komives) in the 1962 Quaker City Festival final . . . Watching the Hawks topple a haughty Wichita State team two years later, a loss that prompted Shocker mentor Gary Thomson to say he'd never bring a team into the Palestra again . . . Seeing Villanova take down a terrific Tennessee team in the Quaker City in '71 . . . The Temple 1969 NIT champs . . . The uncrowned champion La Salle team of '68–69 . . . Villanova scaring UCLA in '71 . . . The great Penn teams and "DON'T FOUL BILSKY AND WOHL!" . . . Villanova 90, Penn 47 . . . Penn going to the Final Four in '79 . . . On and on it goes, right through Marvin O'Connor nearly bringing down Stanford.

And the coaches. Al Severance, who never subbed if he could help it . . . Ken Loeffler . . . Harry Litwack . . . Howie Dallmar . . . Dr. Jack. That's all you need: Dr. Jack . . . Dick Harter . . . Chuck Daly . . . Daddy Mass . . . Paul Westhead . . . Don Casey . . . Jimmy Lynam . . . Bob Weinhauer . . . John Chaney . . . I'm getting goosebumps.

How about the 1966–67 76ers? A 48–4 start? And the '82–83 team that won 65 games while starting Marc Iavaroni? What's up with that? Ah, The Doc, Douggie, Andrew, Bobby and My Man, Maurice Cheeks, the quintessential selfless point guard. Now there is Iverson, the 22nd-century point guard.

God bless Philly. And make mine cheese widdout (Geno's. Don't ask me why.).

— *Bob Ryan*
The Boston Globe

Chapter Five
The High Schools

Where So Many Have Passed with Flying Colors

TED SILARY

If all our city had ever done to make high school basketball better was spawn Wilt Chamberlain, that would have been enough.

But Philadelphia has done much more. As has his alma mater, Overbrook.

Chamberlain, universally considered the Best Player Ever until Michael Jordan came along (and even after, by many), graduated in 1955. The program did not shrivel and die.

Just three years later, the Hilltoppers' starting lineup included three stars — Wayne Hightower, Walt Hazzard and Wali (then Wally) Jones — who would go on to play 31 years in the NBA.

In all, 12 'Brook products have played in The League. Angelo Musi was first, in 1946–47. Malik Rose (Charlotte, then San Antonio) is in his seventh NBA season.

Our city is so amazing, one guy soared all the way to all-timer status, making the NBA's 50-year team in 1997, even though he never played scholastic hoops. That was South Philly's own, Paul Arizin, who went to La Salle High, then blossomed at Villanova.

We've produced many other legends, of course.

Earl "The Pearl" Monroe? He played at John Bartram. Tom Gola? La Salle. Guy Rodgers? Northeast (old building, 8th and Lehigh). Ray "Chink"

Scott? West Philadelphia. Larry Foust, one of the NBA's first competent big men (double-figure average in points 10 times; in rebounds six times)? He attended the old South Catholic (now St. John Neumann).

Roman Catholic and Clayton "Stink" Adams (11), passing by the arm of Jim Schultice, lost to North Catholic in the 1987 Catholic League title game.

DAILY NEWS FILE PHOTO

These days, our headliners include Portland's Rasheed Wallace (Simon Gratz), Houston's Cuttino "Cat" Mobley (Cardinal Dougherty), the Sixers' own Aaron McKie (also Gratz) and Toronto's Alvin Williams (Germantown Academy). Houston's Eddie Griffin (Roman Catholic) is on the doorstep.

Kobe Bryant, star guard with the Los Angeles Lakers, officially is not considered a Philadelphia product because he attended high school (Lower Merion) in the suburbs. But we just want you to know he's "almost" from here, as is guard Dajuan Wagner, who is also likely headed for NBA stardom. Wagner attended Camden High, right across the Ben Franklin Bridge in New Jersey, and was drafted by the Cleveland Cavaliers.

However, perhaps our spirit is best typified by Emanual "Vel" Davis.

Davis was a 6-1 forward at a high school with a subterranean profile, Kensington. While growing to 6-5, he then played for a lowlight college program at Delaware State and scrambled through various minor leagues until earning his dream shot in the NBA in the fall of 1996, at age 29. Just 13 games into a stint with the Houston Rockets, he tore the anterior cruciate ligament in his right knee. He worked like a madman to come back, and at age 33 is still in the NBA with Atlanta.

Our acknowledged city leagues include 56 schools — 34 in the Public, 16 in the Catholic, six in the Inter-Ac.

One thing we're not proud of: allowing a tradition to die. From 1939 through '80, the Public and Catholic champs met for the city title. (The Inter-Ac, made up of private schools, does its own thing and doesn't even have playoffs.) The city title series ended — in all sports, not just basketball — when a girls' coach at a Public League school tried to force the Catholic League to add girls' sports to the menu. Hissed at being bullied, the Catholic League backed away from the table.

Stories That Have Become Legendary

• Several coaches did this: While practicing to play Wilt Chamberlain's Overbrook teams, they set up a table near the basket and had a manager stand on top, using a broom to block shots.

• In 1985, Kensington's game with Frankford was halted with 16 seconds remaining because Kensington had just one player remaining. The Tigers, wracked by academic ineligibility, had just five players in uniform. Four fouled out. Coach Sonny Edelman said he had an inbound play set up for the situation: "We called it, 'Get the ball in to yourself.'"

• In the early 1970s, students at Bishop Kenrick, in Norristown, dribbled all the way to the Palestra to celebrate their school's playoff appearance.

• In the late 1960s, each West Philadelphia Speedboy wore one white sneaker and one black sneaker. Chuck Taylors, of course. The idea was to confuse defenders. (And be oh-so-cool.)

• In the summer of 1990, using an assumed name, Overbrook's Isaiah "Reese" Montgomery won $6,000 in dunk contests sponsored by a beer company. He was then cleared to play that winter by the school district.

Calling Cards

Top 10 memorable nicknames

1. Anthony "Hubba Bubba" King, William Penn, 1982
2. Angel "Fuey" Gonzalez, Edison, 1999
3. Darin "Munchy" Mason, Mastbaum, 1984
4. Sam "Wobbles" White, University City, 1974
5. Vincent "Ham Head" Mason, University City, 1988
6. Bryant "Sad Eyes" Watson, Franklin, 1987
7. Dwayne "Sugar" Hill, Roman, 1993
8. James "Slurp" Gambrell, Edison, 1980
9. Thomas "Skimoe" Hinton, University City, 1989
10. James "Bruiser" Flint, Episcopal, 1983

King of the Adopted Names

Anthony "Hubba Bubba" King, William Penn, Class of 1982

Well-built, lefthanded small forward. Could get to the basket on anyone. Decent mid-range shooter.

Anthony "Hubba Bubba" King

How he got the nickname.

"Playing at Ridgeway Rec [Broad and Christian] when I was 14. First it was Bub, then [Southern High star] Jody Johnson changed it to Hubba Bubba. He'd say something like, 'Hubba Bubba, his dunks cause trubba.'"

Biggest high school thrill.

"Lots of those, man … Go with when I set the [still standing] school record with 50 against Lincoln."

Biggest high school disappointment. (The very next game.)

"Losing out on my chance for the scoring title to 'Bris' [teammate Jerome Brisbon. Penn's senior class trip was the day before the finale. King came late to school and was held out of action by coach Ralph Rice. Brisbon, a junior, scored 40 points to finish with a 28.4 average. King's was 27.3.]. That changed my career. I could have gone to a Big 5 school. Those coaches lost faith in me. They thought I was irresponsible."

College career. (He became famous for bouncing around.)

"How many schools did I go to? [Laughs.] Six or seven. I found my home at Shaw. I was co-MVP of the CIAA with A.J. English."

Grass still doesn't grow under his feet.

"I've got two jobs. I'm a counselor for juvenile delinquents and a security guard."

Still hoopin' after all these years.

"I'm still playing [at 37]. Pretty much four leagues at a time. In the fall I won MVP in a 35-and-over league at Marian Anderson Rec Center [17th and Fitzwater]. It keeps my body in some kind of shape. I've got four kids — two sons, two daughters. I'll have to be ready to teach them the game. I don't dunk as much now, but I'm still winning scoring titles, still winning championships, still winning MVP honors. [Laughs.] I'm one of the few guys this age who can still play the game to perfection."

— Ted Silary

From Nary a Peek to NBA peak

After being cut four times in high school, Paul Arizin's career took off

The Paul Arizin story is Philadelphia legend. Basketball Hall of Famer. Ten-time NBA All-Star as a Philadelphia Warrior, with a 22.8 career scoring average. One of the greatest players, if not the greatest college player, in city history. The 6-4 center from South Philadelphia averaged 20 points in his three seasons at Villanova, including a senior year (1949–50) averaging 25.3 and being selected player of the year.

Paul Arizin

DAILY NEWS FILE PHOTO

All from a man who never played while a student at La Salle High. Arizin was cut at La Salle four times. Legend has it that Villanova head coach Al Severance first heard about Arizin from a coaching friend who had seen the kid from South Philly chewing up Philly's finest schoolboys and college players in independent leagues during his freshman year at Villanova in 1946.

Yellow newspaper clippings tell the story of Severance first seeing Arizin playing for a South Philly all-star team against a group of Villanova players in 1947.

"He did things none of my Villanova players could do," Severance was quoted as saying. "I found it hard to imagine him never playing high school basketball."

"I hadn't gone out for the freshman team, because I wasn't a high school player, and I knew there were a bunch of returning players that year," said Arizin, a Springfield resident. "I went there to be a student. I thought I could play, but after not playing in high school, it wasn't my focus anymore."

After seeing Arizin win MVP honors for The Hastings Club team in a citywide tournament, Severance approached and offered a spot on the team. The rest is history.

"I guess I'm proof that in sports, nothing is impossible," Arizin said.

— *Kevin Mulligan*

There's No Place Like This Home

Unique doesn't begin to describe the Dobbins gymnasium

There is no such thing as a bad basketball experience in the wild and wacky gym at Murrell Dobbins Tech.

You could literally not watch one bounce of a ball and still come away painting word pictures for weeks for your buddies.

Where does one begin?

• With the scoring/timing box. It's about six feet off the floor and tucked into a window on the Lehigh Avenue side. The kids have to step onto a chair to hoist themselves into it and their legs dangle down while they're sitting. Like being in a ski lift.

• With the "fireplaces." They're not really fireplaces, but that's what they look like. They're brick and they go to the ceiling and when the place was built in the 1930s, they must have helped with ventilation. They're in the northeast and northwest corners. One juts out onto the court, so shots from the exact corner are impossible. They're padded, slightly. You still don't want to bump into one.

Some Dobbins features include curtains that hang a few feet off the floor.

JENNIFER MIDBERRY / DAILY NEWS

• With the curtains. They're in the windows on the 22nd Street side and they extend from ceiling to maybe four feet from the floor. They're nice now, but in the mid-1980s they were badly tattered and one of them became dislodged during a game, causing a delay until the sun moved behind the houses across the street.

• With your ears. This place is noisy if two kids are playing one-on-one and nobody else is around. With 50 people it's a madhouse. With a full house and a great game, it sounds as if jets were taking off and landing non-stop.

• With Yank. Rich Yankowitz has been coaching the Mustangs since the 1971–72 season. He always puts on a good show. Try to count how many times he yells, "Be patient!" Don't be surprised if you reach four figures.

• With the cheerleaders/pep squad. In some seasons, it seems like every girl in the school is involved. Or is it only those whose screaming is guaranteed to provide headaches?

The place is named for Hank Gathers, a star for the 1985 Public League champs. He collapsed and died in 1990 while playing for Loyola Marymount.

Though the popular name for the gym is Hank's House, Hank's Madhouse or Funhouse would be much more on target.

— Ted Silary

Other Dobbins features include a brick barrier that straddles the end line and a suspended scoring table.

JENNIFER MIDBERRY / DAILY NEWS

Capitalizing on Punishment

North's JV, subbing for the varsity, shockingly wins a playoff game

On February 26, 1968, a high school playoff game in Philadelphia generated national attention. North Catholic's junior varsity, subbing for the suspended varsity, defeated Bishop McDevitt, 77–60, in a Catholic League quarterfinal before 5,495 at the Palestra. All members of the 12-man varsity (North was the defending city champion) were disciplined for returning late to school after being given permission to eat breakfast at a nearby diner.

Here are 10 tidbits concerning that historic game:

> ### I Remember
>
> So many great recollections . . . playing at West Philly High [1939–42] and Penn [Class of '50] and coaching at Springfield [Montco], but my most exciting memories are of coaching all the great Philly players in the Eastern League [Sunbury] and practicing at 4th and Shunk to get ready. Coaching great players such as Jack Ramsay, Jack McCloskey, John Chaney, Bob Gainey, Jerry Rullo, Jackie Moore, Sonny Hill, Bob Herdelin, "Pickles" Kennedy, Ernie Beck, Paul Senesky, Jim Huggard, Jim Mooney, Howie Landa, Al Guokas and many, many more. So many great friendships and memories of Philly basketball.
>
> *STAN NOVAK*
> *Former NBA scout and Penn Hall of Famer*

1. North's JV had only split with McDevitt's JV during the regular season.

2. The JV guys hadn't played for eight days. They received official notice they'd be needed at 3:30, practiced briefly (some had to borrow sneakers and socks), wolfed down a quick dinner (at the same diner), then rode the El to the Palestra.

3. On the El, one player joked, "People will read about this in the comic strips, not the sports section."

4. North's players were booed by the school's fans as they took the floor. They also heard chants of "We want the varsity! We want the varsity!"

5. McDevitt had one lead, 2–0. North scored the final 11 points.

6. McDevitt's headliner, guard Bobby Haas, had scored 51 points in a regular-season game vs. Ryan, breaking the Catholic League record of La Salle's Joe Heyer. The *Bulletin*'s headline: "Haas nets record 51— 2 higher than Heyer." Ryan, a new school, had no seniors that year.

7. North rang up a 62–36 rebounding advantage, led by Mike Kaiser (23), Iggy Brodzinski (18) and Jim Boylan (15). The guards were ballhandler Billy Dever and sniper Joe Evanosich. Kaiser (20) and Brodzinski (19) led in points.

8. North's coach, Jack Friel, was also the disciplinarian. He said, "We had to show the kids in the most forceful way possible that they were students first, athletes second."

9. The response of the suspended players' parents was mostly positive. "The only guy I really remember being hot was Mr. Siemiontkowski," said JV coach Fran Dougherty, now the school's athletic director. Hank Siemiontkowski, the team's star, went on to play at Villanova. "We saw him that night. I thought he was going to pop us. And he was a *big* man."

10. Two of the JV guys, Kaiser and Dever, saw action six days later in the semifinal, a 51–49 loss to Cardinal O'Hara that came on Lou Ferro's buzzer-beating tip. The ball rolled around the rim for two seconds, then fell in. O'Hara went on to win the championship.

— Ted Silary

Shoot, You Couldn't Make These Stories Up

Top 10 scoring-related games that deserve mention

1. Reggie Isaac
Bartram, *1986*
In an orchestrated attempt by his outgoing coach, John Dougherty, to break Wilt Chamberlain's city record for points in a game (90), Isaac shot 33-for-69 and 18-for-22 for 84 points in a 99–69 win over Bodine. Isaac's teammates were under orders not to shoot. They got off eight shots anyway.

2. Shawn Newman
Dougherty, *1990*
In a preseason game against West Catholic, he shot 21-for-45 (four treys) and 12-for-18 for 58 points — the most ever by a Catholic League player — in a 118–108 win at West Catholic. West's coach, Joe Donahue, came to the *Daily News* with the videotape so the numbers could be verified.

3. Wilt Chamberlain
Overbrook, *1955*
Scored 90 points vs. Roxborough after getting 74 earlier that season against the same opponent and 71 the year before.

4. Rich Conboy and Manny Carlis
Carroll, *1983*
Conboy (24) and Carlis (22) did all of the Patriots' scoring in a 46–41 win at St. Joseph's Prep. Their teammates went 0-for-12 from the floor and 0-for-2 at the line.

5. Troy Daniel
Lamberton, *1984*
Outdueled Engineering and Science's Michael Anderson, 55–32, in a last-day battle for the Public League scoring title. Anderson missed the team bus and was late arriving for the game. Daniel also had 19 rebounds, but no assists. "Oh, well," he said. "You can't have everything."

6. Tom Tobin, *Carroll*, and Brian Pearce
St. Joseph's Prep, *1993*
In 70–51 win for Carroll, Tobin bombed away for nine threes (in 13 attempts) and Pearce nailed eight (in 16 attempts).

7. Na'im Crenshaw, *Overbrook*, and Lynn Greer
Engineering and Science, *1997*
In different games, Crenshaw (38 points) outlasted Greer (45, with nine treys) to win the Public League scoring title, 26.3 to 26.1. Kelli Greer, Lynn's sister and Crenshaw's girlfriend, said the next time Na'im visits, "He might have to stand out on the porch."

Engineering and Science's Lynn Greer barely missed the league scoring title in 1997.

JIM MACMILLAN / DAILY NEWS

8. Marty O'Donnell
North Catholic, *1986*
On December 1, in a 53–49 loss to visiting Gratz, he became the first player in city history to convert a three-point field goal. A deep sub, he left the team shortly thereafter.

9. Craig and Charles Wise
Central, *1990*
Became the first teammate brothers in city history to average 20 points per game. Craig, a junior, averaged 21.3. Charles, a senior, had a 21.0 norm.

10. Willie Taylor, *Olney*, and Joe Bryant
Bartram, *1972*
On the next-to-last day of the Public League season, Bryant scored 57 points vs. Bok to take the lead for the scoring title. On the last day, Taylor scored 63 points vs. Bok to win the title, 28.3 to 27.4.

— Ted Silary

Slick Southpaws

Five top lefties from the past 25 seasons

1. Lynn Greer
Engineering and Science, *1997*

2. Tony Costner
Overbrook, *1980*

3. Brian Daly
Monsignor Bonner, *1988*

4. Rasheed Brokenborough
University City, *1995*

5. Cuttino Mobley
Dougherty, *1992*

Five Performances for the Books

(Playoff games only)

1. Bill Lindsay
West Catholic, *1953*
In a 54–42 win over Overbrook for the city title, he shot 12-for-13 and 8-for-11 for 32 points and was responsible for covering four players as his teammates surrounded Wilt Chamberlain.

2. Donnel Feaster
West Philadelphia, *1997*
The 5-8 sophomore scored 19 of his 38 points in the final quarter as the Speedboys beat Franklin, 78–76, in a Public League round-of-16 game, overcoming a 73–60 deficit in the last 1:27. Dribbled the length of the court for the winning layup at 0:03. Also set a city postseason record with seven three-pointers.

Donnel Feaster scored 38 in a 1997 playoff game vs. Franklin.

DAVID MAIALETTI / DAILY NEWS

3. Paul Terrell
Dougherty, *1974*
Scored 30 points, including 10 in the final quarter, as the Cardinals stunned 16–0 North Catholic, 44–43, in a Catholic League quarterfinal. Terrell shot 14-for-22 from the floor. His teammates shot 5-for-27.

4. Brian Daly
Monsignor Bonner, *1988*
Shot 12-for-14 at the line en route to 30 points as the Friars beat North Catholic, 62–59, for the Catholic League championship. Scored 38.1 percent of his team's points in three playoff games.

5. Craig Wise
Central, *1991*
Collected 46 points, 15 rebounds, five assists and seven steals as the Lancers edged West Philadelphia, 82–80, in a Public League quarterfinal, advancing to a semi for the first time since 1965.

Incarnation Got Gola Started

Tom Gola, a 1951 La Salle High graduate, is considered one of the greatest scholastic basketball players in Philadelphia history. He then went on to stardom at what was then La Salle College, and in the NBA. He was inducted into the Basketball Hall of Fame in 1975. Here's a deeper look at this legend's early days.

Tom Gola was the consummate all-around player.

DAILY NEWS FILE PHOTO

He grew up living at 5110 N. 3rd Street, near Lindley, and attended Incarnation School, 4th and Lindley. He was a fifth grader when he began playing basketball.

"I was an altar boy. One day one of the priests, Father Joseph Belz, took all the altar boys to the gym and had us shoot baskets. I kind of liked it. I went out in my back yard and nailed a peach basket to a post. I started out shooting a beach ball into it."

When Gola was an eighth grader, "Inky" lost to St. Athanasius for the championship of La Salle's grammar school tournament and later beat that same foe in the citywide tournament.

"La Salle offered me and two other guys a scholarship. That was when the high school was where the college still is, at 20th and Olney. I made it through [academically]. The other guys bombed out. Sometimes I'd walk up there or ride my bicycle. Or else I'd take the 47 and 26, or the J bus. La Salle was private. Otherwise I'd have been at North Catholic. [Cardinal Dougherty did not yet exist.] I don't think North even knew I was supposed to go there. They had so many kids anyway. They didn't need me."

Wilt Chamberlain always said that Gola, four years ahead of him in school, was a hero to him. Who was Gola's hero?

"Our coach at Incarnation, Lefty Huber, used to take us to see the 1947 Philadelphia Warriors. That was the start of the NBA. They were the first champions. Joe Fulks, Howie Dallmar, Ed Sadowski, Angelo Musi and George Senesky. That was the starting five. I patterned myself after Howie Dallmar. He had what they called a 'glider shot.' He'd come right down the lane and jump for an underhand layup."

In 1950, with Gola the only junior in the eight-man rotation, La Salle won the Catholic League and city titles. Its only loss came in a postseason tournament. Gola averaged a record 18.9 points in league play.

"When you win a city championship, that's the best you can do. That was a lot of fun."

In 1951, the Explorers lost to St. Thomas More (closed in 1975) in a semifinal. Gola averaged 25.7 points.

"We just couldn't hack it that year. That was disappointing."

One of Gola's more vivid high school memories is off the wall.

"When I was a freshman at La Salle High, I was still playing for Incarnation [CYO team consisting of high school kids]. One day Lefty came in and said we were going to scrimmage North's JV. So we went down there and we were really kicking their butt. [Varsity coach] Phil Looby walks in. He sees what's going on and he sits down and starts to coach. We still kicked their butt. We go back to the locker room and Father 'Knobby' [Thomas Walsh, director of discipline] walks in. He asks Lefty, 'What school do your kids go to?' Lefty tells him, 'Tom here goes to La Salle. The rest of them go to North.' Father Knobby says, 'They go here?! Why didn't they go out for the team?' One of the kids says, 'We did. We were all cut.' . . . That was the problem back then. There were so many kids at tryouts, if you went in and missed your first layup, you were gone. There was one Incarnation kid on that North JV team. He got cut from our team."

— *Ted Silary*

Eddie Griffin helped Roman to successes in the late 1990s.

GEORGE REYNOLDS / DAILY NEWS

97

Philly's All-Time Players

First Team

Wilt Chamberlain
Overbrook, 1955

Tom Gola
La Salle, 1951

Gene Banks
West Philadelphia, 1977

Rasheed Wallace
Simon Gratz, 1993

Eddie Griffin
Roman Catholic, 2000

Second Team

Guy Rodgers
Northeast, 1953

Andre McCarter
Overbrook, 1971

Ray "Chink" Scott
West Philadelphia, 1956

Wayne Hightower
Overbrook, 1958

Walt Hazzard
Overbrook, 1958

Third Team

Lionel Simmons
Southern, 1986

Michael Brooks
West Catholic, 1976

Jerome "Pooh" Richardson
Franklin, 1985

Larry Cannon
Lincoln, 1965

Donnie Carr
Roman Catholic, 1996

Overbrook's Wayne Hightower

For One Weekend, Wilt Was a Player Without a Team

After winning nearly 300 varsity basketball games, after being a successful principal and now as an instructor in the Philadelphia Community College and coaching ninth grade girls' basketball at Archbishop Carroll High School, my mind still continually drifts back to that magical time when I coached Wilt Chamberlain.

My life took a dramatic turn in 1953 when I was appointed head basketball coach at Overbrook High School at the age of 23. The wins and championships are somewhat blurred, but certain events during that time will never be erased from my mind. I read about Larry Brown and his conflicts with Allen Iverson and I empathize with him. Larry is demanding and principled with his beliefs about dedication and cooperation, and a no-nonsense attitude among his players. Stars have a way of testing coaches.

In the 1950s, Wilt was a youngster who was destined for

The 1954–55 Overbrook High city champions, selected Philadelphia's all-time best high school team. Left to right, front row: manager Ted Wexler, Doug Leaman, Martin Hughes, Tom Fitzhugh, Jordan Goldman. Across the back row: Alan Weinberg, Irv Jaffe, David Shapiro, Wilt Chamberlain, Vince Miller, James Sadler, Howard Johnson, coach Cecil Mosenson.

COURTESY OF CECIL MOSENSON

stardom. He was 6-11 with a wingspan of 72 inches. His hands from wrist to fingertip measured $9^1/_2$ inches, so that his hand held a basketball as though it were a grapefruit.

The dunk shot was scarcely known until Wilt came along. With his ability to go $2^1/_2$ feet higher than the rim, and with his great strength, he could ram the ball down into the net with such force that sometimes he ripped the net. Since there was no goaltending rule, Wilt could roam the lane and swat the ball as it approached the basket. The crowds went wild.

Wilt was a prankster, and in his junior year, he had a strong dislike for authority. That junior year, not long into the season, we had our first run-in. It happened during the Frankford game. During the warmups, I was talking to the other coach and the officials when I happened to glance at Wilt. He had adorned himself with a golf cap, a shimmering white silk scarf and dark sunglasses. I called him over and told him very directly to get rid of those glad rags. We went into our pregame huddle, but he kept looking the other way and apparently not listening to me. The game was three minutes old when I realized what was happening. Wilt was angry and was refusing to shoot. I called a timeout and discussed the matter. I got no response so I pulled him out of the game. I gave him a few choice words at the half but only got a sullen stare. I put him into the game and I yanked him out and this went on until the last few minutes of the game when he decided to score and we won the game, although it was very close. I had a private session with him after the game and we had an understanding about what was expected. It worked, because the next game he scored 71 points. This was the first of a few conflicts that established a better relationship between us.

Wilt scored 74 points early in his senior season. We all knew that we were going to play that same team a second time. The game was going to be in the Overbrook gym, which only seated 300 people. The Friday before the game, the practice was lousy since everyone was whooping it up for a new Chamberlain record. I called the team together and told them we were not going to humiliate the other team. Wilt fairly blazed with unspoken defiance. His belligerence was so obvious that it had to be dealt with. I whirled on him and said, "If you don't like the way I'm running the team, you can take a walk." He got up and left the gym. I started practice again, using plays that did not include his presence.

I went to the principal and said, "You better prepare a UPI [United Press International] and an AP [Associated Press] press release. I just threw Chamberlain off the team." I thought that he was going to faint. His response was, "Let's wait until Monday and maybe something positive will happen."

It was a long weekend. I realized that I had just thrown the greatest high school player in the country off the team.

On Monday, I saw Wilt several times in the hallways and he looked the other way. He walked straight past me. At practice time, I walked into the gym

---

I Remember

Wilt had been traded from the Warriors back to Philly [January 15, 1965], and they had a game against the Knicks that night in New York, and to show you how the NBA has changed, they were practicing at a high school in Upper Darby . . . I was working at WDAS, and I asked them if I could cover sports. I saw it as another way of getting on the air. So I went over and when Wilt came out, I walked with him to the bus, and I remember that I would ask Wilt a question, then I would extend the mike as high as I could . . . and he'd say "my man," and then the answer. He always called everyone "my man" if he didn't know your name. But he was very gracious and I got in three or four questions . . . it was just sorta comical . . . I was the only radio reporter there . . . and I'm trying to keep up with Wilt's long stride trying to ask questions.

WDAS had a basketball team and we used to play sometimes before the Sixers game, and I remember Wilt was the scorekeeper for one game. By then he knows my name because he has to put notations next to it, and I had just . . . got three or four taps before I got the basket, and as I'm running past him upcourt, I heard him yell to me, "My man, I got all four of those rebounds."

ED BRADLEY
CBS's 60 Minutes

and there was the big guy shooting baskets. His face was completely expressionless. As I stood looking at him, he approached me with a ball in his hands. I could not imagine what was coming next. He put the ball into my hands and after a pause, asked me if I would help him with his hook shot.

The crisis was over. However, I needed to go to my athletic director and tell him that when we play this team again there is a possibility of a national record, at the expense of this other team. I was uncomfortable about that prospect, but I needed to be fair to Wilt. His advice was that records are broken all the time and since he was a track coach, his analogy was that he doesn't tell his sprinters to slow down when they are winning.

At halftime, Wilt had 26 points, and it was clear now that our relationship was where it should be.

I told him that if he can break the record, he had my blessing. When I took him out with $2^1/_2$ minutes remaining in the game, he had 90 points. He had scored 64 points in $13^1/_2$ minutes. At one point, he scored 15 points in 1 minute.

We spent his senior season visiting many schools around the country. Phog Allen of Kansas was the most persistent and sold Wilt on Kansas.

The rest of his accomplishments are legendary, but of all of his accomplishments, Overbrook High School was the place where he wanted to be best remembered.

— *Cecil Mosenson*

Greatest All-Time Teams

1. Overbrook 1954–55 (18–1)
Wilt Chamberlain averaged 47.2 points in Public League play, scoring 74 and 90 vs. Roxborough. Beat West Catholic for city title, 83–42.

2. Overbrook 1957–58 (22–0)
Featured three future pros in Walt Hazzard, Wayne Hightower and Wali Jones. They played 31 total seasons in the NBA.

3. Simon Gratz 1992–93 (31–0)
Won by an average of 69–39 in Rasheed Wallace's senior season. Defeated Roman, the Catholic League champ, 60–29, in an early-season matchup.

4. West Philadelphia 1976–77 (25–0)
The headliner, Gene Banks, was named national player of the year by several organizations. Among those he beat out for the honor: Magic Johnson.

5. Overbrook 1978–79 (34–1)
All five starters received Division I scholarships. In time, the most celebrated player was the lone junior starter, 6-10 Tony Costner.

6. Murrell Dobbins Tech 1984–85 (28–2)

In the playoffs, future pro Bo Kimble shot 51-for-65 (78.5 percent) from the floor. Doug Overton also made the NBA. Hank Gathers would have, but he collapsed and died while playing with Kimble at Loyola Marymount in 1990.

7. Simon Gratz 1990–91 (27–1)

Levan Alston, Contrell Scott and Shawn "Reds" Smith all were capable of handling pressure. Wallace, a soph, earned first-team All-City honors.

8. Roman Catholic 1990–91 (28–3)

The South MVP was guard Marvin Harrison, now of the NFL's Indianapolis Colts. Average division score: 83–48. Average playoff score: 77–45. Third of six consecutive title teams.

Hank Gathers (left) and Bo Kimble carried Dobbins to a 28–2 record during the 1984–85 season. Both attended Loyola Marymount, which Kimble used as a springboard to the NBA. Gathers collapsed and died while in college in 1990.

DAILY NEWS FILE PHOTO

9. La Salle 1949–50 (24–1)

The headliner was junior Tom Gola, who became a first-magnitude college star and played 11 years in the NBA. Gola set a league record for scoring average (18.9).

10. Bishop Neumann 1964–65 (22–1)

Won its 14 division games by an average of 20.4 points. In the city title game, the Pirates dumped 26–0 Lincoln and future pro Larry Cannon, 75–66.

A View from the Outside

Palestra a "Think Tank for Coaches ... a Player's Proving Ground"

Until the early 1990s, a mysterious door under the [Palestra's] north stands led to the Historical Archaeology Lab of Penn's University Museum. There, unbeknownst to the good burghers of Panicsville overhead, heaps of chips of china and fragments of flower pots for graduate students to clean, tag, and catalog. "Sure, you've got to 'study a few relics,'" I could imagine a crotchety usher saying. "You buy a ticket just like everybody else." So archaeology grad students avoided working on game nights. But on other occasions, with the Palestra at rest, they could hear the cracking of the joists when the heat went down and the clanking of the pipes when it went up again — noises that kept them company.

Perhaps those apprentice archaeologists came across the remains of some of the highly ranked teams interred over the years beneath the famous floor: Western Kentucky, with Jim McDaniels and Clarence Glover, upset by La Salle in 1971; Wichita State with Nate Bowman and Dave Stallworth, upset by St. Joe's in 1964; Bowling Green, with Nate Thurmond and Howard Komives, also upset by the Hawks, in 1962. It was preposterous that West Catholic High should have beaten Wilt Chamberlain and Overbrook High for the 1953 city title, yet after practicing all week with someone standing on a card table under the basket, the Burrs did so, at the Palestra.

Over the years, asking Philadelphians to account for these miracles on 33rd Street, I'd heard many theories. Some people pointed to the great rollers of noise and energy sent back and forth by 9,000 people sitting elbow to elbow, in four banks, in so intimate a space. (The Palestra didn't have a capacity so much as a lawful occupancy.) Those who had spent the most time in the building credited ghosts, risen from the 19th-century potter's field on which the place was built. But I'd always been partial to the theory that the upsets were karmic payback to the home fans, who generously applauded visitors who played well and, arriving early to watch warmups, counted in an audible whisper in 1965 as Bill Bradley dropped in practice shot after practice shot — 26 straight, legend has it.

At its heights the Palestra was as much a think tank for coaches as a player's proving ground. [Jack] Ramsay, [Jim] Lynam, Chuck Daly, Mike Fratello, Harry Litwack, Jack McCloskey, Jack McKinney, Al Severance, Paul Westhead, and Dick Harter all advanced to the NBA, the Hall of Fame, or both. One night in the early 1970s, with his La Salle team trailing Duquesne by 24 points and the Dukes holding the ball, Westhead sent two defenders ahead to the opposite foul line and ordered the

Explorers into a three-man zone. The idea — to make it impossible to Duquesne not to shoot — worked so smartly that La Salle wound up losing by only two. No wonder Ramsay, the coach's coach, always said that winning the City Series meant more to him than winning a national title ever could.

— *Alexander Wolff*

From the book Big Game, Small World: A Basketball Adventure *by Alexander Wolff. Copyright © 2002 by Alexander Wolff. Reprinted by permission of Warner Books, New York, NY. All rights reserved.*

Chapter Six

The Playground

A Breeding Ground for Stars, a Stage for Any Who Rise to It

TED SILARY

No one knew his real name. No one much cared.

"New York" (his original hometown, supposedly) created a partial sensation with his jumpin' exploits during mid-1980s summer league games at Mill Creek Playground, 48th and Brown, in West Philadelphia. He saved the full-blown sensation for afterward.

New York's specialty was jumping over cars. Not the hood part. Not the trunk part.

The middle part.

That's how it is in playgrounds. The sideshow often out-importants the show.

Don't just make a basket and expect to receive love. Drive around two guys — in splashy fashion, of course — then jump over a third to slam while leaving a sneaker imprint on his chest.

"For some players," said Littel Vaughn, a playground/summer league guru based in North Philly, "it's all about getting that 'street credibility.' That's the most important thing in their life. That gets 'em the girls."

Ask many guys who played in college, even in big-time programs, and they'd likely tell you summer leagues in their very own neighborhoods meant more than those wintertime games.

Fans at college games are mostly faceless. In the 'hood, everybody knows everybody and memories are long. Woe the star who gets abused by a no-name. Ten, 15 years of building a rep? Right down the drain.

Philly teems with playgrounds where the action — both official and unofficial — is hot.

Tenth and Lombard in South Philly. 57th and Haverford (Wilt got his start there) and 52nd and Parkside in West Philly. Three along Diamond — at 8th, 25th and 33rd — in North Philly. Upsal and Mansfield in West Oak Lane . . .

Playground games, whether halfcourt or fullcourt, are usually played to 16 points by ones. If it's crowded, the first to 16 wins. If not, the winner often has to prevail by two. Halfcourt games sometimes feature the make-it, take-it rule, which allows the scoring team to keep possession. That's when it's not a good idea to have unmotivated defenders on your squad. Unless, of course, they're very good at fillin' it up and can keep your squad on the court for hours.

Vaughn and Rodney Wescott are the co-commissioners of the Cory Erving Summer League, held at 52nd and Parkside and renamed in 2000 after Julius Erving's deceased son.

"That's the hot one now," Vaughn said. "All the players come through."

A few other summer leagues also have great reputations, but they receive no publicity (and don't seek it, either) because they're not sanctioned by the NCAA and college players sometimes suit up.

In 1980, the *Daily News* published a story about people who stayed up all night playing basketball.

One of the stops on the tour was Marian Anderson Rec Center, at 17th and Fitzwater in South Philly. At 3:17 a.m., a three-on-three game was raging and the language was blue.

Row houses were maybe 50 feet away.

"Everything's cool with the neighbors," said Jeffrey Philson, watching and waiting his turn. "We wanna play some ball, we play some ball. They wanna eat some pig's feet, they eat some pig's feet."

I Remember

For me, it's about people, and in no particular order, those strongest memories go all the way back to [Wilt] Chamberlain. Ironically, we lived on the same street, Salford Street. He lived north of Market, I lived south of Market. When I was a kid [I] remember going to a playground across from Overbrook High School, watching those guys play pick-up games and hoping to get in before the sun went down.

And the [names] aren't restricted to the great players. It's also the great coaches, Coach Litwack and Coach Ramsay, thinking of the many great games and the great moments watching them. The referees, the dear friends who aren't with us now, Joe Gushue and Earl Strom, people I had a great off-the-court relationship with. It's very difficult to pick one thing. Some people will say "We beat Villanova in '65 by the score of . . . ," I don't remember that. But someone gives me a vignette, an incident that happened, then it's right there.

JIM LYNAM
Portland Trail Blazers assistant coach
St. Joe's and Big 5 Hall of Fame

The Courts of Record

City playgrounds where you'll find the top pickup games

1. Hank Gathers Rec Center, 25th and Diamond
Named after the former Dobbins Tech star. Used to be known as Moylan Rec. Former legends who played here are Wilt Chamberlain, Guy Rodgers, Wali Jones, Ray "Chink" Scott and Dawn Staley.

2. 33rd and Diamond
Hosts some of the top outdoor leagues in the area. Pickup games are top-notch.

3. 16th and Susquehanna
Lionel Simmons, Doug Overton, Bo Kimble and Gathers all skilled their games here. Since 1980, home of North Central Philadelphia Basketball League, founded by Omjasisa Kentu.

4. Belfield Rec Center, 20th and Chew
Players of all ages can get good runs here, both outdoor and indoor.

5. Haddington or Shepard Rec Center, 57th and Haverford
Sonny Hill and Chamberlain played here. Usually has games going just about every day when area schools let out. Good winter leagues and good-sized gym.

6. 52nd and Parkside
Home of the Cory Erving Summer League, named after Dr. J's son who died in a car accident.

7. 8th and Diamond
Some of the top pickup runs in the city. Legends who played here include Timmy Brown and Munchy Mason.

8. 22nd and Lehigh
Down the street from the site of what was Connie Mack Stadium, although those who run there now probably never heard of it.

9. Shuler Playground, 27th and Clearfield
Home of the Paul King League.

10. 10th and Lombard
South Philly's hottest pickup games are played here.

11. 34th and Haverford
Mantua Rec Center pulls in some top athletes.

12. 57th and Haverford
Wilt got his start here.

(Contributions from Littel Vaughn and Sonny Hill)

— *Bob Cooney*

Skinny on Dress Code: It Started with the Sneaks

In the early 1950s, the style for playground basketball players was pretty basic: pair of sneakers, shorts and perhaps a shirt, depending if you were on the shirts or skins team.

The only real fashion statement is the sneakers.

"Man, some guys were lucky enough to have Chuck Taylors, but not a lot. If you had them, you were doing all right," city basketball guru Sonny Hill said.

The shoe, made by Converse, was made from canvas and was the most popular sneaker for basketball players of all ages for many, many years.

Playground apparel has come a long way since players simply divided between shirts and skins.

DAILY NEWS FILE PHOTO

"The cost was $3.95 to $5.95, and they were great sneakers," Hill said. "They worked for Wilt Chamberlain, Elgin Baylor, Guy Rodgers and everyone else in that era. And those guys played hard, indoors and out. But then came the leather sneaker and Chuck Taylors weren't good enough for people anymore."

Sneakers, from high top to low, from canvas to leather, from Converse to Nike, have had the biggest impact on playground fashion.

Remember in the early 1980s when Julius Erving and Larry Bird did those silly Converse commercials ("Take two of these and call me in the morning")?

And Bird and Magic Johnson promoting the Converse All-Star sneakers during their great rivalry in the mid-to-late 1980s?

Then along came a guy named Jordan, and Nike took over the top spot with their million varieties of Air Jordans. You also had the Reebok shoe with the pump built into the tongue, adidas making its comeback of late with the retro three-striped look, and scores of others trying to catch the eyes of the modern-day player.

Shorts and socks have changed as well. Gone is the Dr. J look of the tight shorts running only to mid-thigh, with the white socks pulled up to the knee. It is the no-socks look, with knee-length shorts that, for some reason, players like to fall down past their waist, showing off their boxers (another fashion trend this writer cares not to explore. Whatever happened to jock straps, anyway?).

Other trends that have come and gone and come back again are head-bands, Afros, wristbands (although not always worn around the wrist) and, in some cases, the knee-high socks. Can a return of Chuck Taylors be far behind?

"I don't see why not," Hill said. "They were the best shoe ever made because they were so light. The leather sneakers are a lot heavier than the ones we wore when we were younger. But what do I know? I'm an old man."

— Bob Cooney

Once the Other Guy, Now a Legend All His Own

Sonny Hill shoveled a lot of snow in his younger days.

He wasn't looking for spending money. Nor was he doing a favor for the little old ladies in his neighborhood at 16th and Dauphin.

No, Hill's shoveling expertise was honed on the basketball courts that littered the city during his teenage years.

"That was legendary, shoveling the courts so we could get in some runs," Hill said. "The winter was a great time to play outdoors because the courts wouldn't be as crowded as they were in the warmer weather."

Sonny Hill learned his basketball trade on the playgrounds of Philadelphia. His tools — sneakers, a basketball and a pair of legs — carried him to all parts of the city, searching for the best games and the premier players.

"I started playing at Moylan Rec Center, at 25th and Diamond [now known as the Hank Gathers Rec Center]. It was the Mecca of the playground courts," said Hill, now 65. "The year was 1951 and the center had just opened. The games there were great and we tested our skills there all the time.

> ### I Remember
>
> I think Philadelphia has always been a great environment for basketball players. I have tremendous memories of playing outdoor basketball and playing in summer leagues at a couple of places, including 58th and Kingsessing, where I played in a summer league when I was in high school. Just all the great players that came out of Philadelphia made it fortunate for me to grow up there.
>
> *GEOFF PETRIE*
> *President, basketball operations, for Sacramento Kings*
> *Former Springfield-Delco, Princeton, NBA star*

"At one end of the court you would have the younger players, about 13- to 16-year-olds, trying to make a name for themselves so they could go and play on the other end, where the older guys played. You had to wait your turn, that's the way it was. When you got good enough to play with the older guys, you needed to win to keep playing, or you were done."

As Hill got older, he started to explore other parts of the city.

"I did a lot of traveling back then," he said. "We'd go from North Philly to West Philly and play at 57th and Haverford. We'd go to South Philly and play at 19th and Reid or 4th and Shunk. We'd play in Narberth, or A and Champlost, 26th and Master. You name it, we played there. We'd walk if we could or ride public transportation. We had a ball and our sneakers, all we needed was a court."

Playground basketball back then was serious business. Word of a good player would hit the streets, and Hill and his idol, Guy Rodgers, would get to the court as fast as they could, challenging the new big-name player or anyone else they could find.

Sonny Hill relaxes courtside at Temple's Liacouras Center. His namesake league plays its games nearby at McGonigle Hall.

ALEJANDRO A. ALVAREZ / DAILY NEWS

"Guy was so good back then that we would take on five guys, just the two of us. And we'd win. He was great. I was just a year younger, but I carried his bag for him. I knew how special he was, even back then. I was smart enough to sit back and learn from someone who is one of the greatest of all time."

Other greats that Hill dribbled, passed, shot, sweated and bonded with on the city's courts included Wilt Chamberlain, John Chaney, Earl "The Pearl" Monroe, Wali Jones, Ray "Chink" Scott, Hal Lear, Walt Hazzard and many, many more.

"The great part about that era was that as good as everyone was, they all wanted to teach the younger players about the game, to carry on the tradition," Hill said. "I learned so much about the game from watching the guys on the playground.

"You have to remember, we didn't have television back then, so we didn't learn the game from watching the guys on TV. We learned from what was passed down to us from the guys in the neighborhoods. I was playing and trying to emulate Guy Rodgers, John Chaney, guys I played against. Now you have kids trying to play like Allen Iverson and Kobe Bryant and Vince Carter."

It's a situation that doesn't sit well with Hill.

"Things are so structured now with AAU ball and all the leagues that kids get into at such an early age," he said. "My basketball education was taught to me on the streets, in the playgrounds. I'd get home from school and go out and play as long as I could. Today, kids have more on the table. I don't think they have that burning competition feeling that we had when we were young.

"The Philly game of basketball was handed down to me when I was young from guys that also learned about the game on the street. You don't get that a lot now. Kids are playing inside all the time. They are missing out on the whole playground experience."

And shoveling experience. Not a lot of snow in indoor gyms.

— *Bob Cooney*

Grand Slammers

Best of the contemporary playground dunkers

Darin "Munchy" Mason, early 1980s
Laurence "L" Pembrook, early 1990s
Isaiah "Reese" Montgomery, early 1990s
Dominique Stephens, late 1980s
Kurk Reed, late 1980s
Antoine Brockington, late 1990s

— Littel Vaughn

Contemporary Honor Roll

Top Ballhandlers
Aaron "A.O." Owens (1998–present); Rodney "Hot Rod" Odrick (1991–98); Joe Newton (1994–99); Clayton "Stink" Adams (1987–93); Marshall Taylor (1986–91); Darrell "Heat" Gates (1985–92); Jerome "Pooh" Allen (1991–2001); Bounce with Me (present)

Top Team, 1980s
Pipers, coached by Paris Hines. This team had Hank Gathers, Lionel Simmons, Greg "Bo" Kimble, Larry Stewart, Doug Overton and many other stars. They were so loaded that Overton and Stewart didn't start. Won numerous 16th Street titles.

Top Team, 1990s
Toss It Up. They won four 16th Street titles during the '90s.

Top Team, 2000s
Miami Hurricanes, led by Cuttino Mobley, Sean Colson, Tyrone "Crone" Garris and James Spears

Chatting at a recent dunking contest are Laurence Pembrook (left) and Isaiah Montgomery.

STEVE FALK / DAILY NEWS

All-1980s Team
Lionel Simmons; Jody Johnson; Hank Gathers; Rico Washington; Darin "Munchy" Mason; Anthony Chennault; Darrell "Heat" Gates; Calvin Gambrell

All-1990s Team
Bryant "Sad Eyes" Watson; Kareem "Smooth" Townes; Anthony "Hubba Bubba" King; "Hot Rod" Odrick; Titti Branch; Kelvin "Yama" McLeod, tallest player in the city at 7-2; Jerome "Pooh" Allen; Emanual "Vel" Davis; Fred "Crime Dog" Crawford

All-2000s Team
Owens; Garris; Curtis "Dunker" Reed; Shawn Harvey; Ronald "Flip" Murray; Ralphie "Sensational" Holmes

Top Moves
Owens (running crossover); Allen (one-handed crossover); McLeod (sky hook); Bryant Watson (fadeaway); Stephen Stewart (Mookie ball)

Top Announcers
Bill "Buck James" Claiborne (16th and Susquehanna); Charles Dickens (52nd and Parkside); Larry Jones (33rd and Diamond)

(Contributions by Littel Vaughn, coordinator of Elite Sports Youth program in Philadelphia, and Omjasisa Kentu, North Central Philadelphia Basketball League coordinator)

Legends of the Summer Leagues

Wilt Chamberlain
Began playing against Big 5 stars as a 15-year-old in several summer leagues, most notably Narberth. The Overbrook legend played at Narberth most summers during his Kansas career.

Tom Gola
The La Salle College legend was the marquee attraction during the summers of 1951 to 1955.

Guy Rodgers
The Northeast High product packed them in wherever he played from 1955 to 1958, introducing many Narberth League spectators to their first glimpse of ballhandling wizardry.

Ray "Chink" Scott
One of the early West Philly superstars, dazzled pros and collegians after leading the Public League in scoring in 1956.

Paul Arizin
Carved his reputation in independent summer action after not playing high school ball. Became Villanova's greatest player and one of the NBA's 50 Greatest.

Wali Jones
He was called "Wonder" before starring at Villanova. One of several Overbrook legends from the 1958 unbeaten championship team.

Michael Brooks
From West Catholic to La Salle University and 1980 college player of the year honors.

Gene Banks
Arguably West Philly's greatest drew record crowds to see him every summer before he headed to Duke in 1977.

Walt Hazzard
Teamed with Wali Jones and Wayne Hightower against all comers in the late 1950s and early '60s.

Lionel Simmons
Legendary Sonny Hill League product from South Philadelphia, La Salle's all-time leading scorer and 1990 college player of the year.

Earl Monroe
Picked his spots, but when the John Bartram legend showed for summer games, he left them howling.

Best of the Rest (as selected by Philly legends)

1940s
Ernie Beck (West Catholic); Joe Hannan (South Catholic); Larry Faust (South Catholic); Paul "Hook" Wallace (Overbrook); Joe Lang (Northeast); "Buddy" Donnelly (La Salle); Stan "Loady" Brown (Southern); John Gillespie (St. Joe's Prep); Larry Goldsborough (Overbrook)

1950s
Jackie Moore (Overbrook); Hal "Hotsy" Reinfeld; Guido "Dippy" Carosi (Overbrook); Claude Gross (Ben Franklin); Hubie White (West Philadelphia); John Chaney (Ben Franklin); Hal Lear (Overbrook); Jim "Tee" Parham (Northeast); Sonny Hill (Northeast); Ace McCann (Bartram); Bob McNeill (North Catholic); Clarence "Bud" Houck (Lincoln); Joe Heyer (La Salle); Jack Wallin (St. Thomas More); Bill "Pickles" Kennedy (Lincoln)

1960s
Jim Huggard (West Catholic); Jimmy Lynam (West Catholic); Larry Cannon (Lincoln); Frank Corace (Bonner); Matt Guokas (St. Joe's Prep);

Mike Bantom (Roman); Billy Hoy (St. Thomas More); George Sutor (Father Judge); Mike Hauer (Bonner); Bruce Drysdale (Lincoln); Billy Oakes (St. John Neumann)

1970s

Andre McCarter (Overbrook); Rich Laurel (Overbrook); Joe Bryant (Bartram); Chico Singleton (Roman); Joe Gore (Simon Gratz); Joe Anderson (Simon Gratz); Lewis Lloyd (Overbrook); Milt Colston (Olney); Bill Magarity (Cardinal Dougherty); Maurice Howard (St. Joe's Prep); Emery Sammons (St. Thomas More); Reggie Jackson (Roman)

1980s

Michael Anderson (Engineering & Science); Jerome "Pooh" Richardson (Franklin); Tony Costner (Overbrook); Bo Kimble (Murrell Dobbins); Timmy Brown (Jules Mastbaum); Brian Shorter (Gratz); Lonnie McFarlan (Roman); Rodney Blake (Bonner); Charles Hickman (Episcopal); Anthony Chennault (Frankford); Kevin Beaford (Bok)

1990s

Rasheed Wallace (Gratz); Carlin Worley (Frankford); Marvin O'Connor (Gratz); Lynn Greer (Engineering & Science); Marc Jackson (Roman); Martin Ingelsby (Archbishop Carroll); Donnie Carr (Roman); Rasual Butler (Roman); Cuttino Mobley (Dougherty); Eddie Griffin (Roman)

A long-ago game at 56th and Christian draws an interested gathering.

INQUIRER PHOTO

Courts Put Town on Map

On doorstep of city, Narberth League has played to all comers

Mention summer league basketball to a Philly-area legend — from Paul Arizin to Earl Monroe to Gene Banks, from the 1940s to the present — and chances are good that you'll find yourself talking about Narberth.

The Narberth League and Philly basketball seemingly have been joined at the conversational hip since the summer action began on, yes, concrete-like dirt courts in Narberth in the early 1940s.

"If you were a great player or wanted to see a great player, Narberth was the place to be," said Bill White, a former director of the league located at Narberth Playground, in the heart of the Main Line off Haverford Avenue. "They came from everywhere, coaches, players and spectators. And once they experienced it, they kept coming back. It was pure Philly basketball and every night, it was the best Philly had to offer."

> ### I Remember
>
> I remember as a kid, going to the Palestra, seeing Bill Bradley, the greatest experience of life . . . walking in as an assistant coach at Rutgers, all the history and tradition. It still troubles me, maybe the greatest player I've ever seen on TV, Guy Rodgers, who is no longer with us, still isn't in the Hall of Fame. When I think of Philly I think of the Sonny Hill League, all the great coaches: John Chaney, Harry Litwack, Jack Kraft at Villanova. I can remember going to see Villanova play against [Niagara's] Calvin Murphy. There's just so much history . . . when I was in the NBA . . . coaching in there, coming in with the Pistons, it's just a special city. Even the high schools, all the great players that the City and Catholic Leagues have produced over the years.
>
> *DICK VITALE*
> *ESPN*

Wilt Chamberlain played there. Paul Arizin. Guy Rodgers. Wayne Hightower. Tom Gola. Walt Hazzard. The Pearl, Earl Monroe, before he became "The Pearl." And on and on and on. The stories told decades later by former players and coaches are legendary.

There was the summer of '67, White recalled, when a 7-2 high school senior from Dotham, Alabama, and a 6-8 forward from Sarasota, Florida, lived with Villanova assistant coach George Raveling while playing at Narberth for his team named Three Country Boys, featuring Villanova players. The high school kids were Artis Gilmore (who went to Jacksonville) and Howard Porter, whom Raveling landed for coach Jack Kraft.

In 1974, while in hot pursuit of Springfield-Delco's 6-9 Dave Batton, University of Kentucky coach Joe Hall chartered a bus full of Kentucky boosters to attend a Batton Narberth game. "I'm not sure what the recruiting rules were back then," White said, "but he apparently couldn't speak to Dave, but he wanted to make an impression, so he had every one of them wearing Kentucky jerseys in the bleachers. It was a sea of blue. You couldn't miss it." Batton went to Notre Dame.

Most summers, Narberth offered a preview of the upcoming Big 5 seasons, until the point-shaving scandals of 1961 brought NCAA regulations and a ban on college players performing in summer leagues. In 1962, Narberth turned its focus to the high school players, who found the two lighted, paved courts from neighborhoods throughout Philadelphia and the suburbs. As the premier high school summer league, it was not uncommon to see 10 or 15 of college basketball's most famous coaches eyeing talent in crowds that often swelled toward 800 for the nightly (Monday to Thursday) doubleheaders.

"It was like watching sold-out Big 5 doubleheaders every night," said Billy Oakes, the NBA official and former St. Joe's guard. "It was like the Palestra outdoors. The intensity was unmatched. And once spectators found a spot, you didn't move. Because you couldn't."

Narberth's success spawned summer leagues throughout the city that grew in popularity as Philly basketball exploded in the '50s and '60s. Courts at 25th and Diamond, A and Champlost, 4th and Shunk, and Haddington Recreation Center (52nd and Parkside) all produced a long line of legends. In 1960, former Eastern League star Sonny Hill founded competing summer leagues for all ages, including post-college professionals (Charles Baker League). Hill's leagues, now including girls and boys from junior high (Futures) to college, continue to be a positive influence on city youth on many levels, including academics, as the city's modern-era, premier place for summer competition.

— Kevin Mulligan

A View from the Outside

"Sunday in the playgrounds as far away from this earth as the sanctified people in the storefront churches"

The game resumes. Splat of the ball dribbled, grunts and yells as the players jostle for position under the backboards, work themselves free for shots and passes. An older player, chunky, bearded, head shaven clean, bulls his way through the lane for a lay-up. A lean, black boy guarding him springs high, his hand at least a foot above the rim, but all he can do is slap his palm against the metal backboard because the other's shot has already looped around his flailing arm and ricocheted through the goal. The entire standard, orange rim, steel poles, the perforated metal backboard continue to shudder after the action has passed. Littleman liked the way the thick, yellowish man had made his move. No waste of energy. Everything for go, nothing for show. The man was past walking on air, past the rubber legged dunking and pinning shots on the backboard which made the gallery squeal, hoot and shake their heads. But the man knew the game. How to conserve his strength, how to use his bulk to offset the spring of long muscled jumping jacks he contested for rebounds. A kind of fluid inevitability when he drove for the basket. He was going to get his no matter how high the others jumped, no matter what impossible refinements their skills brought into the game.

Sunday morning, barely ten thirty, but the sun was already high and the court crowded. A rainbow of colors, jerseys advertising high schools, churches, hamburger shops, real estate agencies, garages, clubs, colleges, a few emblazoned with pro or semi-pro names, but dominating these was the spectrum of flesh tones from dull ivory to glistening black, the wet muscles highlighted by brilliant sunshine. Littleman wondered how they had survived, the sleek muscles, the strength, the pride, how did it bloom again and again, how were these men so real, so richly full of life. Where did it hide the six days a week they were trapped in the decaying city? How did the vigor, the beauty disguise itself, how did these men slip into the nonentity, the innocuousness demanded of them as they encountered the white world. Black men playing basketball. Less than half of them were high school or college athletes. Most had to be classed as dishwashers and janitors or men who carried mail, men who scuffed to make ends meet for themselves and their families. Yet here they were. Playing this game the way it should be played. Sunday in the playgrounds as far away from this earth as the sanctified people in the storefront churches just down the block, singing and shaking their way to glory.

— *John Edgar Wideman*

John Edgar Wideman is a Philadelphia native and two-time winner of the PEN/Faulkner Award. At Penn, he was All-Ivy and an All-Big 5 player and a Rhodes scholar. This passage is from The Lynchers *(Harcourt Brace Jovanovich, 1986).*

Chapter Seven

The Quiz

Take a shot at this 50-question quiz on Philadelphia basketball

1. During the 1976–77 regular season, six different members of the Sixers had high games of 32 points or more. Name them.

2. Who was La Salle's leading scorer when La Salle topped Villanova without the injured Kenny Durrett on February 13, 1971?

3. Who was the last St. Joseph's player drafted by an NBA team?

4. Only one father-son combo has won the Markward Award as the city's top senior basketball player. Name them.

5. The players who hold the top three slots for most three-point field goals in an NBA season by a rookie have strong Philadelphia connections. In fact, they were all rookies the same season. Name the players and the season.

6. Who holds La Salle's single-game scoring mark?

7. Which Philadelphia Warrior twice shot 0-for-15 from the floor in a game?

8. From 1991–92 to 1996–97, the Sixers finished with a different leading scorer every season. Name them.

9. Three different players hold the Temple scoring records for career, season and game. Who are they?

10. Which former Penn player coached the Quakers for three seasons in the mid-1980s?

11. Who led the 1966–67 NBA champion Sixers in assists during the regular season?

12. The players who made up the Drexel backcourt in 1986–87 and '87–88 are now first and second on the school's career assists list. Name them.

13. True or false: No Sixer has ever won the NBA's slam dunk or three-point shooting contest at the All-Star Game festivities.

14. From 1969 to 1974, Drexel and West Chester played in the same league as La Salle, Temple and St. Joseph's. Name it.

15. At what Public League school did Harry Litwack and John Chaney, who went on to coaching fame at Temple, get their X-and-Oing starts?

16. Which fouled-out Hawk did Steve Donches replace before hitting his famous game-winning shot in the 1966 Villanova game?

17. A Penn player has scored 40 points in a game three times. Ernie Beck did it twice, scoring 47 and 45. Who was the third, with a 44-point game?

18. Which one-season Sixer tied an NBA record with 16 free-throw attempts in the fourth quarter of a December 13, 1994, game?

19. Georgetown beat Villanova twice during the 1985 regular season before falling to the Wildcats in the NCAA championship game. Which of the Wildcats' five other tournament victims also beat them during the regular season?

20. Who did Bernard Blunt pass to become St. Joseph's all-time career scorer?

21. Name any of the four players who came off the bench for the Warriors in Wilt Chamberlain's 100-point game on March 2, 1962.

22. True or false: Villanova has never won the Big East Tournament championship.

23. Name any Sixers first-round pick from 1967 to 1971. We'll even give you their colleges: BYU, Utah State, Santa Clara, Wisconsin, Tulsa.

24. Who preceded Harry Litwack as Temple's head coach?

25. Which brothers won scoring titles in the Public League and Inter-Ac, respectively, in 1966 and 1971?

26. Who is the only Sixer to lead the NBA in disqualifications?

27. Which team jumped out to a 24–0 lead on Penn en route to a 34-point victory on January 6, 1989?

28. Which two teams did Duke and Kentucky beat at the Spectrum to advance to their magical East Regional final in 1992?

29. Which Sixer won the first NBA Sixth Man Award?

30. In 1959–60, Wilt Chamberlain became the second Philadelphia Warrior to win the NBA's Rookie of the Year Award. Who was the first, having done it two seasons earlier?

31. Name the man who coached different schools to Catholic League championships in back-to-back years.

32. Which team did Temple defeat to win the 1969 NIT championship?

33. The Philadelphia Warriors won two NBA championships. Which two franchises did they defeat in the Finals? Hint: One club is defunct; the other has since moved.

34. In 1984, the year before the NCAA Tournament expanded to 64 teams, there was a tripleheader of play-in games at the Palestra. Name the three winning schools.

35. What were the first names of the two Johnsons who played on the Sixers' 1982–83 NBA championship team?

36. Name the three Sixers head coaches who also coached in an ABA All-Star Game.

37. Michael Anderson has six of the seven triple-doubles in Drexel history. Who has the other?

38. Steve Black led La Salle in scoring his freshman, sophomore and senior seasons. Who led the team in Black's junior year?

39. Larry Brown led the ABA in assists per game in each of its first three seasons. Which Villanova product did so in the following three seasons?

40. Four times a Sixer has led the NBA in minutes played. Wilt Chamberlain did it three times. Who was the fourth?

41. The 1976–77 Villanova Wildcats had three Herron brothers. Name them.

42. Allen Iverson led the NBA in scoring in the 2000–01 season, but he did not record the high game. Which former Sixer did?

43. Which player led Villanova in assists for four consecutive seasons starting in 1985–86?

44. In 1969, three Temple Owls were drafted by both the NBA and the ABA. Name them.

45. Before St. Joseph's toppled No. 1 DePaul in the 1981 NCAA Tournament second round, the team had to win a first-round game. Who did the Hawks beat?

46. In the 1975 draft, the Sixers drafted Darryl Dawkins fifth overall out of which Orlando, Florida, high school?

47. Which Penn Quaker made 10 consecutive free throws down the stretch to help top ninth-ranked Villanova on December 11, 1982?

48. Lionel Simmons won just one NCAA Tournament game in his La Salle career. Ironically, it was over a team that the Explorers had lost to in the NIT final when Simmons was a freshman. Name the school.

49. Who holds Drexel's single-game scoring mark?

50. Who had the highest-scoring game of a Philadelphia Warrior not named Wilt Chamberlain?

Quiz Answers

1. Julius Erving (40), World B. Free (39), George McGinnis (37), Steve Mix (37), Doug Collins (33), Mike Dunleavy (32)
2. Bobby Fields
3. Wayne Williams, 1987
4. O'Hara's Tom Ingelsby won in 1969. Carroll's Martin Ingelsby won in 1997; his dad was his coach.
5. Kerry Kittles (158), Allen Iverson (155) and Matt Maloney (154) in 1996–97
6. Kareem Townes (52)
7. Howie Dallmar
8. Starting with 1991–92: Charles Barkley, Hersey Hawkins, Clarence Weatherspoon, Dana Barros, Jerry Stackhouse, Allen Iverson
9. Mark Macon, Hal Lear, Bill Mlkvy
10. Craig Littlepage
11. Wilt Chamberlain (630)
12. Michael Anderson and Todd Lehmann
13. True
14. Middle Atlantic Conference
15. Both were coaches at Simon Gratz.
16. Billy Oakes
17. Hassan Duncombe
18. Willie Burton
19. Maryland
20. Craig Amos
21. York Larese, Ed Conlin, Joe Ruklick, Ted Luckenbill
22. False. The Wildcats captured the 1995 tourney.
23. In order: Craig Raymond, Shaler Halimon, Bud Ogden, Al Henry and Dana Lewis
24. Josh Cody
25. Buddy Harris at Roxborough, Billy Harris at Penn Charter. Buddy pitched briefly for the Houston Astros.
26. Shawn Bradley, 1994–95
27. Temple
28. Seton Hall and Massachusetts, respectively
29. Bobby Jones, 1982–83
30. Woody Sauldsberry
31. Eddie Burke, St. Joseph's Prep in 1971 and St. Thomas More in '72
32. Boston College
33. Chicago Stags in 1947, Fort Wayne Pistons in 1956
34. Princeton (beat San Diego), Richmond (Rider) and Northeastern (Long Island)
35. Reggie and Clemon
36. Larry Brown, Alex Hannum, Kevin Loughery

37. Casper Cooper
38. Ralph Lewis, 1983–84
39. Bill Melchionni
40. Maurice Cheeks, 1985–86
41. Keith, Larry and Reggie
42. Jerry Stackhouse (57)
43. Kenny Wilson
44. John Baum, Ed Mast, Joe Cromer
45. Creighton
46. Maynard Evans
47. Anthony Arnoli
48. Southern Mississippi
49. John Rankin (44)
50. Joe Fulks (63, February 10, 1949)

Making the Grade

Let's see how much you've been paying attention to the city's last half-century of hoops. We're curious whether your score puts you in the starting lineup or on the bench.

Under 15
Oh, my. Forget practice. Take a couple of laps around the Villanova campus and pop your head into the Jake Nevin Field House.

16–25
And you call yourself a gym rat? Go sit at the knee of La Salle's Bob Vetrone for a day.

26–35
Put on the practice jersey. St. Joseph's Cindy Anderson-Griffin might want to take a look at you.

36–45
Mind playing the point? Tell Temple's John Chaney you deserve a shot.

46–50
Wow! Get ready to jump center. They're already hanging your image on a wall at the Palestra.

Chapter Eight

The Timeline

March 20, 1897: Yale defeats visiting Penn, 32–10, in the first-ever five-on-five basketball game.

1918–19: Eddie Gottlieb's South Philadelphia Hebrew Association (SPHAs) wins the last two championships of the Philadelphia League.

Jan. 1, 1927: Penn opens the Palestra with a 26–15 win over Yale.

1929–31: The SPHAs, led by Temple's Harry Litwack, win three Eastern League titles.

Dec. 9, 1931: La Salle begins play, beating the alumni in a game at Wister Hall.

Jan. 21, 1932: John Chaney is born in Jacksonville, Florida.

1932: In the first-ever game at Villanova Field House, the Wildcats lose to Temple, 29–25.

1933: The SPHAs join the ABL.

Aug. 21, 1936: Wilt Chamberlain is born.

March 16, 1938: Temple beats Colorado, 60–36, to win the men's NIT, the prestigious postseason tournament of that time.

June 6, 1946: The Basketball Association of America (BAA), which would become the National Basketball Association (NBA), is formed.

April 22, 1947: The Philadelphia Warriors defeat the Chicago Stags in five games to win the first BAA title.

1949: After winning seven titles, the SPHAs and the ABL disband.

Aug. 3, 1949: The 17-team NBA is formed.

Nov. 26, 1949: St. Joseph's loses the first-ever game at the Alumni Memorial Fieldhouse, falling to Rhode Island, 62–46.

1950–59

Feb. 22, 1950: Julius Erving is born in Roosevelt, New York.

March 15, 1952: La Salle wins the NIT championship, 75–64, over Dayton in New York.

March 20, 1954: La Salle wins the NCAA Tournament by beating Bradley, 92–76, at Kansas City.

Nov. 23, 1954: The formation of the Big 5 is announced.

Feb. 17, 1955: Overbrook senior Wilt Chamberlain scores 90 points in a 123–21 win over Roxborough, a boys' city record that still stands.

Dec. 14, 1955: St. Joe's beats Villanova, 83–70, in the first City Series game at the Palestra.

April 7, 1956: The Warriors beat the Fort Wayne Pistons, 99–88, to win the NBA championship in five games.

1959: The Warriors use their territorial selection to draft Chamberlain, who had played collegiately at Kansas.

1960–69

Jan. 22, 1960: Philadelphia hosts its first NBA All-Star Game, won by the Eastern Conference. Chamberlain (23 points, 25 rebounds) is the game's MVP.

Nov. 24, 1960: Chamberlain grabs an NBA-record 55 rebounds against Bill Russell and the Celtics.

March 2, 1962: Chamberlain sets an NBA record with 100 points against the New York Knicks in a game at Hershey.

April 5, 1962: The Warriors lose to the Boston Celtics, 109–107, in Game 7 of the Eastern Conference finals. It is the last game for the Philadelphia team, which moves to San Francisco following the season.

May 22, 1963: The NBA approves the franchise move of the Syracuse Nationals to Philadelphia.

Aug. 6, 1963: The NBA approves the name change from the Nationals to the 76ers.

Oct. 16, 1963: The 76ers make their debut by winning at Detroit, 117–115.

Oct. 19, 1963: The 76ers lose their home opener, 124–121, to Detroit.

Jan. 15, 1965: The 76ers acquire Wilt Chamberlain from the San Francisco Warriors for Connie Dierking, Paul Neumann and Lee Shaffer, plus cash.

Jan. 21, 1965: In front of 6,140 at the Arena, Wilt Chamberlain makes his 76ers debut with 22 points, 29 rebounds and 12 blocks in a 111–102 win over San Francisco.

April 24, 1967: The 76ers beat San Francisco in Game 6, 125–122, to win their first NBA title.

Oct. 18, 1967: The 76ers open the Spectrum by defeating the Los Angeles Lakers, 103–87.

Feb. 2, 1968: Wilt Chamberlain notches the NBA's only triple-double-double with 22 points, 25 rebounds and 21 assists in a 131–121 win over Detroit.

July 9, 1968: The 76ers trade Wilt Chamberlain to the Los Angeles Lakers for Jerry Chambers, Archie Clark and Darrall Imhoff.

Dec. 2, 1969: Temple beats St. John's, 60–59, in the first game at McGonigle Hall.

1970–79

Jan. 20, 1970: The NBA All-Star Game is played at the Spectrum. Willis Reed has 21 points and 18 rebounds to lead the East to a 142–135 win over the West.

March 25, 1973: The 76ers lose to Detroit, 115–96, to finish the season 9–73, the worst record in NBA history.

April 23, 1973: The 76ers select Doug Collins out of Illinois State with the first overall pick.

March 23, 1974: Immaculata defeats Mississippi College, 68–53, to win its third consecutive women's national championship.

June 7, 1975: Allen Iverson is born in Hampton, Virginia.

Feb. 3, 1976: Dave Bing (16 points) is named game MVP after leading the East to a 123–109 win in the NBA All-Star Game, played in Philadelphia.

March 29, 1976: Indiana caps a perfect 32–0 season by beating Michigan, 86–68, to win the NCAA Tournament final at the Spectrum.

Oct. 21, 1976: The 76ers purchase Julius Erving's contract from the New York Nets of the ABA.

June 5, 1977: After leading the NBA Finals, 2–0, the 76ers lose four games in a row to Bill Walton and the Portland Trail Blazers.

Nov. 3, 1977: Billy Cunningham is named 76ers coach.

March 18, 1979: Penn beats St. John's, 64–62, to advance to the Final Four.

1980–89

May 16, 1980: The 76ers lose to the Lakers in the NBA Finals, 4–2. Rookie Magic Johnson scores 42 points in the final game.

Feb. 13, 1981: Dobbins Tech's Linda Page scores 100 points, a Philadelphia high school record, in a 131–37 win over Mastbaum.

March 14, 1981: St. Joe's defeats No. 1–ranked DePaul in one of the most stunning upsets in NCAA Tournament history. John Smith's layup gives the Hawks the 49–48 win.

March 28–30, 1981: Philadelphia plays host to the NCAA Final Four, again won by Indiana, which beats North Carolina, 63–50, in the championship.

May 3, 1981: The 76ers blow a 3–1 series lead and lose to the Celtics in Game 7 of the Eastern Conference finals.

July 8, 1981: Harold Katz purchases the 76ers from Fitz Dixon.

June 8, 1982: For the second time in three years, the 76ers lose the NBA Finals to the Los Angeles Lakers in six games.

Sept. 15, 1982: The 76ers acquire Moses Malone from the Houston Rockets for Caldwell Jones and a No. 1 pick.

May 31, 1983: Capping one of the greatest seasons in league history, the 76ers sweep the Lakers to win the NBA title.

June 19, 1984: The 76ers draft Charles Barkley with the fifth overall pick.

April 1, 1985: Eighth-seeded Villanova completes a miraculous six-game run by beating heavily favored Georgetown, 66–64, to win the NCAA championship.

Feb. 1, 1986: Villanova begins play at the Pavilion with a 64–62 victory over Maryland.

June 6, 1986: It is announced that Big 5 games are no longer to be held exclusively at the Palestra.

1990–99

Feb. 22, 1990: La Salle's Lionel Simmons scores his 3,000th career point. Simmons, the national player of the year in 1990, ends his career with a city college record 3,217 points.

March 4, 1990: Hank Gathers, a Loyola Marymount star and Dobbins Tech product, collapses on the court during a West Coast Conference Tournament game. He is pronounced dead two hours later.

May 13, 1991: The format for the Big 5 schedule is reduced to a half round-robin.

March 28, 1992: Duke defeats Kentucky in overtime, 104–103, to win the East Region of the NCAA Tournament at the Spectrum. Christian Laettner's buzzer-beater ends one of college basketball's greatest games.

June 17, 1992: The 76ers trade Charles Barkley to the Phoenix Suns for Jeff Hornacek, Andrew Lang and Tim Perry.

April 24, 1996: The 76ers are sold by Harold Katz to the Comcast Corporation, led by Pat Croce.

June 26, 1996: The 76ers use the No. 1 overall pick to select Allen Iverson.

Nov. 1, 1996: The 76ers begin play at the CoreStates Center, losing 111–103 to the Milwaukee Bucks.

May 5, 1997: The 76ers name Larry Brown coach.

Dec. 9, 1997: Temple beats 18th-ranked Fresno State in the first-ever game at the Forum at the Apollo of Temple.

Dec. 19, 1997: The 76ers acquire Theo Ratliff, Aaron McKie and a first-round pick from Detroit for Jerry Stackhouse, Eric Montross and a second-rounder.

Feb. 21, 1998: La Salle beats Virginia Tech, 74–64, in the first game at the Tom Gola Arena.

May 19, 1998: Billy King is promoted from vice president of basketball administration to general manager of the 76ers.

Dec. 22, 1998: The American Basketball League, the latest women's pro league with a Philadelphia franchise, folds.

Oct. 12, 1999: Wilt Chamberlain dies at age 63.

2000–02

April 2, 2000: No. 1–ranked Connecticut beats Tennessee, 71–52, at the First Union Center to win the women's NCAA Tournament.

Jan. 16, 2001: Camden High's Dajuan Wagner scores 100 points in a 157–67 win over Gloucester Township Tech.

Feb. 22, 2001: The 76ers acquire Dikembe Mutombo from the Atlanta Hawks in a six-player deal.

June 3, 2001: The 76ers defeat the Bucks, 108–91, in Game 7 of the Eastern Conference finals to advance to the NBA Finals for the first time in 18 years.

Oct. 5, 2001: John Chaney and Moses Malone are among those inducted into the Basketball Hall of Fame.

Dec. 8, 2001: All six men's college teams play one another in a tripleheader at the Palestra. La Salle defeats Drexel, 80–70. St. Joe's beats Penn, 67–61. Villanova downs Temple, 70–66.

Feb. 10, 2002: Philadelphia hosts the NBA All-Star Game.

— *Ed Barkowitz*

Statistics and Lists

Professional Statistics

PHILADELPHIA 76ERS, YEAR BY YEAR

Season	Record	Home	Away
1963-64	34-46 (.425)	18-12	16-34
1964-65	40-40 (.500)	13-12	27-28
1965-66	55-25 (.688)	22-3	33-22
1966-67	68-13 (.840)	28-2	40-11
1967-68	62-20 (.756)	27-8	35-12
1968-69	55-27 (.671)	26-8	29-19
1969-70	42-40 (.512)	22-16	20-24
1970-71	47-35 (.573)	24-15	23-20
1971-72	30-52 (.366)	14-23	16-29
1972-73	9-73 (.110)	5-26	4-47
1973-74	25-57 (.305)	14-23	11-34
1974-75	34-48 (.415)	20-21	14-27
1975-76	46-36 (.561)	34-7	12-29
1976-77	50-32 (.610)	32-9	18-23
1977-78	55-27 (.671)	37-4	18-23
1978-79	47-35 (.573)	31-10	16-25
1979-80	59-23 (.720)	36-5	23-18
1980-81	62-20 (.756)	37-4	25-16
1981-82	58-24 (.707)	32-9	26-15
1982-83	65-17 (.793)	35-6	30-11
1983-84	52-30 (.634)	32-9	20-21
1984-85	58-24 (.707)	34-7	24-17
1985-86	54-28 (.659)	31-10	23-18
1986-87	45-37 (.549)	28-13	17-24
1987-88	36-46 (.439)	27-14	9-32
1988-89	46-36 (.561)	30-11	16-25
1989-90	53-29 (.646)	34-7	19-22
1990-91	44-38 (.537)	29-12	15-26
1991-92	35-47 (.427)	23-18	12-29
1992-93	26-56 (.317)	15-26	11-30
1993-94	25-57 (.305)	15-26	10-31
1994-95	24-58 (.293)	14-27	10-31
1995-96	18-64 (.220)	11-30	7-34
1996-97	22-60 (.268)	11-30	11-30
1997-98	31-51 (.378)	19-22	12-29
1998-99	28-22 (.560)	17-8	11-14
1999-2000	49-33 (.598)	29-12	20-21
2000-01	56-26 (.683)	29-12	27-14
2001-02	43-39 (.538)	22-19	21-20

76ERS SCORING LEADERS

Season	Player	Avg. (ppg)
1963-64	Hal Greer	23.3
1964-65	Wilt Chamberlain	30.1
1965-66	Chamberlain	33.5
1966-67	Chamberlain	24.1
1967-68	Chamberlain	24.3
1968-69	Billy Cunningham	24.8
1969-70	Cunningham	26.1
1970-71	Cunningham	23.0
1971-72	Cunningham	23.3
1972-73	Fred Carter	20.0
1973-74	Carter	21.4
1974-75	Carter	21.9
1975-76	George McGinnis	23.0
1976-77	Julius Erving	21.6
1977-78	Erving	20.6
1978-79	Erving	23.1
1979-80	Erving	26.9
1980-81	Erving	24.6
1981-82	Erving	24.4
1982-83	Moses Malone	24.5
1983-84	Malone	22.7
1984-85	Malone	24.6
1985-86	Malone	23.8
1986-87	Charles Barkley	23.0
1987-88	Barkley	28.3
1988-89	Barkley	25.8
1989-90	Barkley	25.2
1990-91	Barkley	27.6
1991-92	Barkley	23.1
1992-93	Hersey Hawkins	20.3
1993-94	Clarence Weatherspoon	18.4
1994-95	Dana Barros	20.6
1995-96	Jerry Stackhouse	19.2
1996-97	Allen Iverson	23.5
1997-98	Iverson	22.0
1998-99	Iverson	26.8
1999-2000	Iverson	28.4
2000-01	Iverson	31.1
2001-02	Iverson	31.4

PHILADELPHIA 76ERS, PLAYOFFS

1963-64
Eastern Division semifinals
Cincinnati 3, 76ers 2

1964-65
Eastern Division semifinals
76ers 3, Cincinnati 1
Eastern Division finals
Boston 4, 76ers 3

1965-66
Eastern Division finals
Boston 4, 76ers 1

1966-67
Eastern Division semifinals
76ers 3, Cincinnati 1
Eastern Division finals
76ers 4, Boston 1
NBA Finals
76ers 4, San Francisco 2

1967-68
Eastern Division semifinals
76ers 4, New York 2
Eastern Division finals
Boston 4, 76ers 3

1968-69
Eastern Division semifinals
Boston 4, 76ers 1

1969-70
Eastern Division semifinals
Milwaukee 4, 76ers 1

1970-71
Eastern Division semifinals
Baltimore 4, 76ers 3

1975-76
First round
Buffalo 2, 76ers 0

1976-77
Eastern Conference semifinals
76ers 4, Boston 3
Eastern Conference finals
76ers 4, Houston 2
NBA finals
Portland 4, 76ers 2

1977-78
Eastern Conference semifinals
76ers 4, New York 0
Eastern Conference finals
Washington 4, 76ers 2

1978-79
First round
76ers 2, New Jersey 0
Eastern Conference semifinals
San Antonio 4, 76ers 3

1979-80
First round
76ers 2, Washington 0
Eastern Conference semifinals
76ers 4, Atlanta 1
Eastern Conference finals
76ers 4, Boston 1
NBA Finals
Los Angeles 4, 76ers 2

1980-81
First round
76ers 2, Indiana 0
Eastern Conference semifinals
76ers 4, Milwaukee 3
Eastern Conference finals
Boston 4, 76ers 3

1981-82
First round
76ers 2, Atlanta 0
Eastern Conference semifinals
76ers 4, Milwaukee 2
Eastern Conference finals
76ers 4, Boston 3
NBA Finals
Los Angeles 4, 76ers 2

1982-83
Eastern Conference semifinals
76ers 4, New York 0
Eastern Conference finals
76ers 4, Milwaukee 1
NBA Finals
76ers 4, Los Angeles 0

1983-84
First round
New Jersey 3, 76ers 2

1984-85
First round
76ers 3, Washington 1
Eastern Conference semifinals
76ers 4, Milwaukee 0
Eastern Conference finals
Boston 4, 76ers 1

1985-86
First round
76ers 3, Washington 2
Eastern Conference semifinals
Milwaukee 4, 76ers 3

1986-87
First round
Milwaukee 3, 76ers 2

1988-89
First round
New York 3, 76ers 0

1989-90
First round
76ers 3, Cleveland 2
Eastern Conference semifinals
Chicago 4, 76ers 1

1990-91
First round
76ers 3, Milwaukee 0
Eastern Conference semifinals
Chicago 4, 76ers 1

1998-99
Eastern Conference semifinals
Indiana 4, 76ers 0

1999-2000
First round
76ers 3, Charlotte 0
Eastern Conference semifinals
Indiana 4, 76ers 2

2000-01
First round
Philadelphia 3, Indiana 1
Eastern Conference semifinals
76ers 4, Toronto 3
Eastern Conference finals
76ers 4, Milwaukee 3
NBA Finals
Los Angeles 4, 76ers 1

2001-02
First round
Boston 3, 76ers 2

PHILADELPHIA 76ERS

ALL-NBA FIRST TEAM
Charles Barkley: 1987-88 through 1990-91
Wilt Chamberlain: 1965-66 through 1967-68
Billy Cunningham: 1968-69 through 1970-71
Julius Erving: 1977-78 and 1979-80 through 1982-83
Allen Iverson: 1998-99 and 2000-01
Moses Malone: 1982-83 and 1984-85
George McGinnis: 1975-76

ALL-NBA SECOND TEAM
Charles Barkley: 1985-86, 1986-87 and 1991-92
Billy Cunningham: 1971-72
Hal Greer: 1963-64 through 1968-69
Julius Erving: 1976-77 and 1983-84
Allen Iverson: 1999-2000
Moses Malone: 1983-84
George McGinnis: 1976-77

ALL-NBA THIRD TEAM
Dikembe Mutombo: 2000-01

MOST VALUABLE PLAYERS
Wilt Chamberlain: 1965-66 through 1967-68
Julius Erving: 1980-81
Allen Iverson: 2000-01
Moses Malone: 1982-83

COACH OF THE YEAR
Larry Brown: 2000-01
Dolph Schayes: 1965-66

ROOKIE OF THE YEAR
Allen Iverson: 1996-97

SIXTH MAN AWARD
Bobby Jones: 1982-83
Aaron McKie: 2000-01

DEFENSIVE PLAYER OF THE YEAR
Dikembe Mutombo: 2000-01

FINALS MVP
Moses Malone: 1983

ALL-STAR GAME MVP
Charles Barkley: 1991
Julius Erving: 1977 and 1983
Hal Greer: 1968
Allen Iverson: 2001

PHILADELPHIA 76ERS

ALL-TIME TEAM LEADERS, SEASON

SCORING AVERAGE

1965-66:	Wilt Chamberlain, 33.5
2001-02:	Allen Iverson, 31.4
2000-01:	Iverson, 31.1
1999-2000:	Iverson, 28.4
1987-88:	Charles Barkley, 27.6

ASSISTS

1985-86:	Maurice Cheeks, 753
1967-68:	Wilt Chamberlain, 702
1981-82:	Cheeks, 667
1987-88:	Cheeks, 635
1966-67:	Chamberlain, 630

REBOUNDS

1966-67:	Wilt Chamberlain, 1,957
1967-68:	Chamberlain, 1,952
1965-66:	Chamberlain, 1,943
1982-83:	Moses Malone, 1,194
1969-70:	Billy Cunningham, 1,101

BLOCKS

1994-95:	Shawn Bradley, 274
1990-91:	Manute Bol, 247
1991-92:	Bol, 205
1997-98:	Theo Ratliff, 203
1976-77:	Caldwell Jones, 200

STEALS

1973-74:	Steve Mix, 212
1981-82:	Maurice Cheeks, 209
1985-86:	Cheeks, 207
1975-76:	George McGinnis, 198
1980-81:	Cheeks, 193

SINGLE-SEASON RECORDS

Total points, 2,649 (Wilt Chamberlain, 1965-66)
Minutes played, 3,836 (Chamberlain, 1967-68)
Average points per game, 33.5 (Chamberlain, 1965-66)
Field goals, 1,074 (Chamberlain, 1965-66)
FG attempted, 1,990 (Chamberlain, 1965-66)
FG percentage, 68.3 (Chamberlain, 1966-67)
3-point FG, 197 (Dana Barros, 1994-95)
3-point FG attempted, 460 (Vernon Maxwell, 1995-96)
3-point FG percentage, 46.4 (Barros, 1994-95)
Free throws made, 737 (Moses Malone, 1984-85)
FT attempted, 976 (Chamberlain, 1965-66)
FT percentage, 93.8 (Mike Gminski, 1987-88)
Rebounds, 1,957 (Chamberlain, 1966-67)
Offensive rebounds, 445 (Malone, 1982-83)
Defensive rebounds, 749 (Malone, 1982-83)
Assists, 753 (Maurice Cheeks, 1985-86)
Personal fouls, 338 (Shawn Bradley, 1994-95)
Disqualifications, 18 (Bradley, 1994-95)
Steals, 212 (Steve Mix, 1973-74)
Blocks, 274 (Bradley, 1994-95)
Turnovers, 350 (Bradley, 1985-86)
Consecutive field goals, 35 (Chamberlain, 1966-67)

PHILADELPHIA WARRIORS, YEAR BY YEAR

Season	Coach	Record	Playoffs
1946-47	Ed Gottlieb	35-25	8-2
1947-48	Gottlieb	27-21	6-7
1948-49	Gottlieb	28-32	0-2
1949-50	Gottlieb	26-42	0-2
1950-51	Gottlieb	40-26	0-2
1951-52	Gottlieb	33-33	1-2
1952-53	Gottlieb	12-57	0-0
1953-54	Gottlieb	29-43	0-0
1954-55	Gottlieb	33-39	0-0
1955-56	George Senesky	45-27	7-3
1956-57	Senesky	37-35	0-2
1957-58	Senesky	37-35	3-5
1958-59	Al Cervi	32-40	0-0
1959-60	Neil Johnston	49-26	4-5
1960-61	Johnston	46-33	0-3
1961-62	Frank McGuire	49-31	6-6

WARRIORS SCORING LEADERS

Season	Name	Avg. (ppg)
1946-47	Joe Fulks	23.2
1947-48	Fulks	22.1
1948-49	Fulks	26.0
1949-50	Fulks	14.2
1950-51	Fulks	18.7
1951-52	Paul Arizin	25.4
1952-53	Neil Johnston	22.3
1953-54	Johnston	24.4
1954-55	Johnston	22.7
1955-56	Arizin	24.2
1956-57	Arizin	25.6
1957-58	Arizin	20.7
1958-59	Arizin	26.4
1959-60	Wilt Chamberlain	37.6
1960-61	Chamberlain	38.4
1961-62	Chamberlain	50.4

College Statistics

VILLANOVA

CAREER SCORING LEADERS

Player	Seasons	Pts.	Avg.
1. Kerry Kittles	1992-96	2,243	18.4
2. Keith Herron	1974-78	2,170	18.5
3. Bob Schafer	1951-55	2,094	18.9
4. Doug West	1985-89	2,037	14.8
5. Howard Porter	1968-71	2,026	22.8
6. John Pinone	1979-83	2,024	16.1
7. Ed Pinckney	1981-85	1,865	14.4
8. Larry Hennessy	1950-53	1,737	23.2
9. Paul Arizin	1947-50	1,649	20.1
10. Alex Bradley	1977-81	1,634	14.7

COACHING RECORDS

Coach	Seasons	Record	Pct.
Michael A. Saxe	1920-26	64-30	.681
John C. Cashman	1926-29	21-26	.447
George W. Jacobs	1929-36	62-56	.525
Alex Severence	1936-61	413-201	.673
Jack Kraft	1961-73	238-95	.715
Rollie Massimino	1973-92	357-241	.597
Steve Lappas	1992-2001	174-110	.613
Jay Wright	2001-present	19-13	.594

POSTSEASON FINALS

1938-39:   NCAA runner-up, lost to Ohio State, 53-36
1964-65:   NIT runner-up, lost to St. John's, 55-51
1970-71:   NCAA runner-up, lost to UCLA, 68-62
1984-85:   NCAA national champion, beat Georgetown, 66-64
1993-94:   NIT champion, beat Vanderbilt, 80-73

ALL–BIG FIVE SELECTIONS

1956:	Jimmy Smith
1957:	Al Griffith
1958:	Tom Brennan
1959:	Joe Ryan
1960:	Jim Huggard, Hubie White
1961:	Jim Huggard, Hubie White
1962:	Wali Jones, Hubie White
1963:	Wali Jones, Jim Washington
1964:	Jim Washington
1965:	Bill Melchionni
1966:	Bill Melchionni
1967:	Johnny Jones
1968:	Johnny Jones
1969:	Johnny Jones, Howard Porter
1970:	Howard Porter
1971:	Howard Porter
1972:	Chris Ford, Tom Ingelsby
1973:	Tom Ingelsby
1976:	Keith Herron
1977:	Keith Herron
1978:	Keith Herron
1979:	Alex Bradley
1980:	Alex Bradley, John Pinone, Rory Sparrow
1981:	Stewart Granger, John Pinone
1982:	Ed Pinckney, John Pinone, Stewart Granger
1983:	Ed Pinckney, John Pinone, Stewart Granger
1984:	Ed Pinckney, Dwayne McClain
1985:	Dwayne McClain, Gary McLain, Ed Pinckney
1986:	Harold Pressley, Harold Jensen
1987:	Harold Jensen, Mark Plansky
1988:	Tom Greis, Mark Plansky, Doug West
1989:	Doug West, Chris Walker
1990:	Chris Walker, Tom Gries
1991:	Lance Miller, Greg Woodard
1992:	Lance Miller, Greg Woodard
1994:	Kerry Kittles
1995:	Kerry Kittles, Eric Eberz, Jason Lawson
1996:	Kerry Kittles, Jason Lawson, Eric Eberz, Alvin Williams
1997:	Alvin Williams, Jason Lawson, Tim Thomas
1998:	Howard Brown, John Celestand
1999:	John Celestand, Malik Allen, Howard Brown
2000:	Malik Allen, Gary Buchanan
2001:	Michael Bradley, Gary Buchanan
2002:	Ricky Wright, Gary Buchanan

TEMPLE

CAREER SCORING LEADERS

Player	Seasons	Pts.	Avg.
1. Mark Macon	1987-91	2,609	20.7
2. Lynn Greer	1997-2002	2,099	15.3
3. Terence Stansbury	1980-84	1,811	15.7
4. Guy Rodgers	1955-58	1,767	19.6
5. Nate Blackwell	1983-87	1,708	13.2
6. Granger Hall	1980-85	1,652	14.4
7. Aaron McKie	1991-94	1,650	17.9
8. Mike Vreeswyk	1985-89	1,650	13.9
9. John Baum	1966-69	1,544	17.9
10. Bill Mlkvy	1949-52	1,539	21.1

COACHING RECORDS

Coach	Seasons	Record	Pct.
Charles W. Williams	1894-99	73-32	.695
John T. Rogers	1899-1900	14-8	.636
H. Shindle Wingert	1901-05	20-18	.526
John B. Crescendo	1905-08	14-10	.583
Edward M. McCone	1908-09	8-3	.727
Fred Prosch Jr.	1909-13	17-20	.459
William Nicolai	1913-17	31-26	.544
Elwood Geiges	1917-18	8-7	.533
Francois M. D'Eliscu	1919-23	30-22	.577
Samuel L. Dienes	1923-26	39-21	.650
James Usilton Sr.	1926-39	205-79	.722
Ernest Messikomer	1939-42	35-27	.564
Josh Cody	1942-52	122-104	.540
Harry Litwack	1952-73	373-193	.659
Don Casey	1973-82	151-94	.616
John Chaney	1982-present	425-181	.701

POSTSEASON FINALS

1968-69:   NIT champion, beat Boston College, 89-76

ALL–BIG FIVE SELECTIONS

1956:   Guy Rodgers, Hal Lear
1957:   Mel Brodsky, Jay Norman, Guy Rodgers
1958:   Jay Norman, Guy Rodgers
1959:   Bill Kennedy
1960:   Bill Kennedy
1961:   Bruce Drysdale
1962:   Bruce Drysdale
1964:   Jim Williams, Bob Harrington
1966:   Jim Williams
1967:   John Baum, Clarence Brookins
1968:   John Baum
1969:   John Baum
1972:   Ollie Johnson
1977:   Marty Stahurski
1978:   Tim Claxton, Michael Stahurski
1979:   Bruce Harrold, Rick Reed
1981:   Neal Robinson
1982:   Granger Hall, Terence Stansbury
1983:   Terence Stansbury, Jim McLoughlin
1984:   Granger Hall, Terence Stansbury, Jim McLoughlin
1985:   Granger Hall, Charles Rayne
1986:   Tim Perry, Nate Blackwell, Ed Coe
1987:   Nate Blackwell
1988:   Howard Evans, Mark Macon, Tim Perry, Mark Vreeswyk
1989:   Mark Macon, Mike Vreeswyck
1990:   Donald Hodge, Mark Macon
1991:   Mark Macon, Don Hodge, Mik Kilgore
1992:   Aaron McKie, Mik Kilgore, Mark Strickland
1993:   Eddie Jones, Aaron McKie, Rick Brunson
1994:   Eddie Jones, Aaron McKie, Rick Brunson
1995:   Rick Brunson
1996:   Marc Jackson
1997:   Marc Jackson, Rasheed Brokenborough, Pepe Sanchez
1998:   Lamont Barnes, Rasheed Brokenborough, Pepe Sanchez
1999:   Lamont Barnes, Pepe Sanchez, Mark Karcher
2000:   Mark Karcher, Pepe Sanchez, Quincy Wadley
2001:   Lynn Greer, Kevin Lyde, Quincy Wadley
2002:   Lynn Greer, David Hawkins

PENN

CAREER SCORING LEADERS

Player	Seasons	Pts.	Avg.
Ernie Beck	1950-53	1,827	22.3
Keven McDonald	1975-78	1,644	20.8
Michael Jordan	1997-2000	1,604	14.7
Ron Haigler	1972-75	1,552	12.0
Jerome Allen	1991-95	1,518	13.5
Stan Pawlak	1963-66	1,501	20.3
Bruce Lefkowitz	1983-87	1,443	13.9
Bob Morse	1969-72	1,381	16.4
Matt Maloney	1991-95	1,370	12.0
Herb Lyon	1945-50	1,333	14.2

COACHING RECORDS

Coach	Seasons	Record	Pct.
R. B. Smith	1905-09	73-22	.768
Charles Keinath	1909-12	36-25	.590
Arthur Kiefaber	1912-14	10-24	.294
Lon Jourdet	1914-20	87-28	.756
Edward McNichol	1920-30	186-63	.747
Lon Jourdet	1930-43	140-42	.769
Donald Kellett	1943-48	46-31	.597
Robert Dougherty	1945-46	7-10	.412
Howard Dallmar	1948-54	105-51	.673
Ray Stanley	1954-56	31-19	.620
Jack McCloskey	1956-66	146-105	.582
Dick Harter	1966-71	88-44	.667
Chuck Daly	1971-77	125-38	.767
Bob Weinhauer	1977-82	99-45	.687
Craig Littlepage	1982-85	40-39	.506
Tom Schneider	1985-89	51-54	.486
Fran Dunphy	1989-present	231-129	.642

POSTSEASON FINALS

None

ALL–BIG FIVE SELECTIONS

1956:	Dick Csencitz, Joe Sturgis
1957:	Dick Csencitz
1958:	Dick Csencitz
1959:	George Schmidt
1960:	Bob Mlkvy
1961:	Bob Mlkvy
1963:	John Wideman
1964:	Ray Carazo, Jeff Neuman, Stan Pawlak
1965:	Jeff Neuman
1966:	Jeff Neuman, Stan Pawlak
1968:	Pete Andrews
1970:	Corky Calhoun
1971:	Corky Calhoun, Bob Morse
1972:	Phil Hankinson, Bob Morse
1973:	Phil Hankinson
1974:	Ron Haigler
1975:	Ron Haigler, Bob Bigelow
1976:	John Engles, Keven McDonald
1977:	Keven McDonald
1978:	Keven McDonald
1979:	Tony Price, Tim Smith
1980:	James Salters
1982:	Paul Little
1983:	Michael Brown, Paul Little
1985:	Perry Bromwell, Karl Racine
1986:	Perry Bromwell
1987:	Perry Bromwell, Bruce Lefkowitz
1990:	Hassan Duncombe, Jerry Simon
1992:	Paul Chambers
1993:	Jerome Allen, Matt Maloney, Barry Pierce
1994:	Jerome Allen, Matt Maloney, Barry Pierce
1995:	Jerome Allen, Matt Maloney
1996:	Ira Bowman, Tim Krug
1998:	Michael Jordan, Paul Romanczuk
1999:	Michael Jordan, Paul Romanczuk
2000:	Michael Jordan, Matt Langel, Ugonna Onyekwe
2001:	Lamar Plummer
2002:	Ugonna Onyekwe, Andrew Toole, Koko Archibong

LA SALLE

CAREER SCORING LEADERS

Player	Seasons	Pts.	Avg.
Lionel Simmons	1986-90	3,217	24.6
Michael Brooks	1976-80	2,628	23.1
Tom Gola	1951-55	2,461	20.9
Rasual Butler	1998-2002	2,125	19.3
Donnie Carr	1996-2000	2,067	19.7
Steve Black	1981-85	2,012	19.7
Kareem Townes	1992-95	1,925	23.8
Randy Woods	1989-92	1,811	20.6
Ralph Lewis	1981-85	1,807	15.6
Doug Overton	1987-91	1,795	14.6

COACHING RECORDS

Coach	Seasons	Record	Pct.
John J. Henry	1930-31	15-4	.789
Thomas Conley	1931-33	28-11	.718
Leonard Tanseer	1933-41	90-59	.604
Charles O'Brien	1941-43	25-21	.543
Joseph Meehan	1943-46	28-30	.483
Charles McGlone	1946-49	61-17	.782
Ken Loeffler	1949-55	145-30	.829
Jim Pollard	1955-58	48-28	.632
"Dudey" Moore	1958-63	79-37	.681
Bob Walters	1963-65	31-17	.646
Joe Heyer	1965-67	24-27	.471
Jim Harding	1967-68	20-8	.714
Tom Gola	1968-70	37-13	.740
Paul Westhead	1970-79	142-105	.575
"Lefty" Ervin	1979-86	119-87	.578
"Speedy" Morris	1986-2001	238-203	.540
Billy Hahn	2001-present	15-17	.469

POSTSEASON FINALS

1951-52: NIT champion, beat Dayton, 75-64
1953-54: NCAA champion, beat Bradley, 92-76
1954-55: NCAA runner-up, lost to San Francisco, 77-63
1986-87: NIT runner-up, lost to Southern Mississippi, 84-80

ALL–BIG FIVE SELECTIONS

1956:	Fran O'Malley
1957:	Tom Garberina, Alonzo Lewis
1959:	Ralph Bantivoglio, Bob Herdelin
1960:	Bob Alden
1961:	Bob McAteer
1962:	Bob McAteer
1963:	Frank Corace
1964:	Frank Corace
1965:	Curt Fromal
1966:	Hubie Marshall
1967:	Larry Cannon, Hubie Marshall
1968:	Larry Cannon, Bernie Williams
1969:	Larry Cannon, Bernie Williams, Ken Durrett
1970:	Ken Durrett
1971:	Ken Durrett, Bobby Fields
1973:	Jim Crawford
1974:	Bill Taylor, Joe Bryant
1975:	Joe Bryant, Bill Taylor, Charlie Wise
1976:	Charlie Wise
1977:	Michael Brooks
1978:	Michael Brooks
1979:	Michael Brooks
1980:	Michael Brooks
1981:	Kevin Lynam
1982:	Steve Black
1983:	Ralph Lewis
1984:	Steve Black, Ralph Lewis, Albert Butts
1985:	Ralph Lewis, Steve Black
1986:	Chip Greenberg
1987:	Tim Legler, Lionel Simmons
1988:	Lionel Simmons, Tim Legler
1989:	Doug Overton, Lionel Simmons
1990:	Doug Overton, Lionel Simmons, Randy Woods
1991:	Doug Overton, Randy Woods
1992:	Jack Hurd, Randy Woods
1993:	Kareem Townes
1994:	Kareem Townes
1995:	Kareem Townes, Paul Burke
1996:	Romaine Haywood
1997:	Donnie Carr, Mike Gizzi
1998:	Donnie Carr, K'Zell Wesson
1999:	Donnie Carr, K'Zell Wesson
2000:	Donnie Carr, Rasual Butler, Victor Thomas
2001:	Rasual Butler, Victor Thomas
2002:	Rasual Butler

ST. JOSEPH'S

CAREER SCORING LEADERS

Player	Seasons	Pts.	Avg.
Bernard Blunt	1990-95	1,985	16.7
Craig Amos	1988-92	1,735	15.2
Tony Costner	1980-84	1,729	14.4
Cliff Anderson	1964-67	1,728	20.6
Maurice Martin	1982-86	1,726	15.1
Norman Black	1975-79	1,726	16.6
Mike Banton	1970-73	1,684	20.0
Bob Lojewski	1981-85	1,682	14.5
Rodney Blake	1984-88	1,679	14.5
Marvin O'Connor	1999-2002	1,678	18.8

COACHING RECORDS

Coach	Seasons	Record	Pct.
John Dever	1909-10	10-6	.625
Edward Bennis	1910-11	6-6	.500
John Donahue	1911-19	78-52	.600
John Lavin	1919-26	50-62	.446
Tom Temple	1926-28	12-22	.353
Bill Ferguson	1928-53	309-208	.598
John McMenimen	1953-55	26-23	.531
Jack Ramsay	1955-66	234-72	.765
Jack McKinney	1966-74	144-77	.652
Harry Booth	1974-78	44-61	.419
Jim Lynam	1978-81	65-28	.699
Jim Boyle	1981-90	151-114	.570
John Griffin	1990-95	75-69	.521
Phil Martelli	1995-present	126-90	.583

POSTSEASON FINALS

None

ALL–BIG FIVE SELECTIONS

1956:	Kurt Engelbert, Mike Fallon, Al Juliana, Bill Lynch
1957:	Dick Dougherty, Kurt Engelbert, Ray Radziszewski
1958:	Bob McNeil
1959:	Bob McNeil, Joe Spratt
1960:	Joe Gallo, Bob McNeil
1962:	Tom Wynne
1963:	Jim Lynam, Tom Wynne
1964:	Steve Courtin, Wally Jones
1965:	Cliff Anderson, Matt Goukas
1966:	Cliff Anderson, Matt Goukas
1967:	Cliff Anderson
1968:	Mike Hauer, Dan Kelly, Bill DeAngelis
1969:	Mike Hauer
1970:	Mike Hauer, Dan Kelly
1972:	Mike Bantom
1973:	Mike Bantom, Pat McFarland
1974:	Mike Moody, Jim O'Brien
1976:	Norman Black
1977:	Norman Black
1980:	Boo Williams
1981:	Bryan Warwick
1982:	Jeffrey Clark, Bryan Warwick, Tony Costner, Lonnie McFarlan
1983:	Bob Lojewski, Tony Costner
1984:	Maurice Martin, Tony Costner, Bob Lojewski
1990:	Craig Amos
1991:	Craig Amos, Rap Curry
1992:	Bernard Blunt, Craig Amos
1993:	Bernard Blunt, Rap Curry, Carlin Warley
1994:	Carlin Warley, Rap Curry
1995:	Reggie Townsend, Carlin Warley
1996:	Reggie Townsend, Mark Bass, Will Johnson
1997:	Rashid Bey, Arthur "Yah" Davis, Dmitri Domani
1998:	Rashid Bey, Harold Rasul
1999:	Andre Howard
2000:	Marvin O'Connor
2001:	Jameer Nelson, Marvin O'Connor, Bill Phillips
2002:	Marvin O'Connor, Jameer Nelson, Bill Phillips

High School Statistics

THE CITY'S 50-POINT CLUB

Pts.	Name	School	Year
90	Wilt Chamberlain	Overbrook	1955
84	Reggie Isaac	Bartram	1986
74	Wilt Chamberlain	Overbrook	1955
71	Wilt Chamberlain	Overbrook	1954
66	Michael Anderson	Eng. & Science	1984
65	Billy Harris	Penn Charter	1971
63	Bill Soens	Penn Charter	1963
	Willie Taylor	Olney	1972
61	Eric White	Bodine	1991
59	Wilt Chamberlain	Overbrook	1954
	Kareem "Rab" Townes	Southern	1991
58	Shawn Newman	Dougherty	1990
57	Mike Moore	Bartram	1968
	Joe Bryant	Bartram	1972
	Rasiheed "Noot" Arnold	Franklin LC	1994
56	Lionel Simmons	Southern	1986
55	Frank Stanczak	Roxborough	1947
	Troy Daniel	Lamberton	1984
	Jai Hill	Girard Coll.	1990
	Kareem "Rab" Townes	Southern	1991
54	Barry Love	Overbrook	1947
	Charlie Zoll	Gtn. Acad.	1954
	Craig Wise	Central	1991
53	Eric White	Bodine	1991
	Rahim Washington	Overbrook	1998
52	Ray Shiffner	Roxborough	1950
	Jim Muldoon	Southern	1954
	Frank Kunze	Bartram	1964
	Gene Banks	West Phila.	1977
	Jai Hill	Girard Coll.	1990
51	Joe Hindelang	Lincoln	1963
	Bob Haas	McDevitt	1968
	Billy Harris	Penn Charter	1971
	Dawan Robinson	King	2000
50	Richie Kohler	Penn Charter	1955
	Anthony "Bub" King	Penn	1982
	Jonathan Haynes	Gtn. Friends	1990
	Anwar Amin	Bodine	1993
	Fred Warrick	Bok	1994
	Abdul Taylor	Audenried	1996
	Lynn Greer	Eng. & Science	1997

DAILY NEWS ALL-CITY TEAMS

1972
FIRST TEAM
Joe Bryant	Bartram
Maurice "Mo" Howard	SJ Prep
Mike Sojourner	G-town
Willie Taylor	Olney
Mike Arizin	O'Hara

SECOND TEAM
Barry Brodzinski	N. Cath.
Mike Stokes	W. Phila.
Sydney Sheppard	Mastbaum
Rich Laurel	Overbrook
Mike Stack	Bonner

THIRD TEAM
Glenn Collier	W. Cath.
Ed Enoch	P. Charter
Charlie Floyd	Malvern
Willie Cooks	Southern
Marty Lee	G-town

1973
FIRST TEAM
Dana Clark	Olney
Barry Brodzinski	N. Cath.
Charlie Floyd	Malvern
John "Chubby" Cox	Roxboro
Jim "Chico" Singleton	Roman

SECOND TEAM
Joe Gore	Gratz
Joe Rogers	Carroll
Steve Vassalotti	SJ Prep
Jim Edwards	Judge
Mike Enoch	P. Charter

THIRD TEAM
Harry Ley	Wash.
Donald Kelly	Roman
Lyric Collier	W. Cath.
Jim Wolkiewicz	N. Cath.
Galen Baker	Mastbaum

1974
FIRST TEAM
Joe Gore	Gratz
Milt Colston	Olney
Charlie Floyd	Malvern
Marvin Brown	Gratz
DeCarsta "Byrd" Webster	G-town

SECOND TEAM
Mike Enoch	P. Charter
Lloyd Ranson	Neumann
Tim Claxton	G-town
Karrington Ward	Franklin
Tony Weldon	Gtn.-Stev.

THIRD TEAM
Phil Andrews	Frankford
John Willcox	Malvern
Rendell Bradley	Bartram
Don Hobson	N. Cath.
John Griffin	Roman

1975
FIRST TEAM
Gary Devlin	Gratz
Zane Major	Roman
Gene Banks	W. Phila.
Rodney Lee	Edison
Tim Smith	W. Phila.

SECOND TEAM
Anthony "Stinky" Norris	Southern
Rodney Duncan	Gtn. Acad.
Greg Joyner	Northeast
Al Clancy	Judge
Michael Brooks	W. Cath.

THIRD TEAM
Joe Kurtz	N. Cath.
Terry Hannan	Bonner
Bob Stephens	Olney
Lawrence Reid	Dougherty
Mark Dwight	W. Phila.

1976
FIRST TEAM
Gene Banks	W. Phila.
Michael Brooks	W. Cath.
Rodney Duncan	Gtn. Acad.
Lawrence Reid	Dougherty
Jim "Mo" Connolly	Judge

SECOND TEAM
Mike Blackshear	Overbrook
Clarence "Eggy" Tillman	W. Phila.
Daryl Wilson	Frankford
Charles Murphy	G-town
Donny Dodds	SJ Prep

THIRD TEAM
Mike Edelman	Hav. Sch.
Gordy Bryan	Malvern
Paul Mulholland	Kenrick
Matt Mihalich	La Salle
Ken Mitchell	Southern
Mike Davis	W. Cath.

1977
FIRST TEAM
Gene Banks	W. Phila.
Clarence "Eggy" Tillman	W. Phila.
Reggie Jackson	Roman
Lewis Lloyd	Overbrook
Jeffery "Monk" Clark	Frankford
Fran McCaffery	La Salle

SECOND TEAM
Darryl Warwick	W. Phila.
Mike Edelman	Hav. Sch.
Gordy Bryan	Malvern
Bob Convey	Judge
Joe Schoen	N. Cath.

THIRD TEAM
Pat Purcell	Malvern
Richard Furr	W. Cath.
Larry Gainey	Bartram
Kevin Fitzpatrick	Ryan
Kevin "Butch" Lynam	Carroll
Neal Robinson	Mastbaum
Dan Hastings	Bonner
Chris Foy	SJ Prep
Joe Garrett	W. Phila.

1978
FIRST TEAM
Clarence "Eggy" Tillman	W. Phila.
Reggie Jackson	Roman
Kevin Broadnax	Southern
Mike Edelman	Hav. Sch.
Ray Thompson	Mastbaum

SECOND TEAM
Horace Owens	Dobbins
Carlton "C-9" Willis	Overbrook
Donny Dodds	St. James
Angelo Reynolds	W. Cath.
Reuben McCoy	Mastbaum

THIRD TEAM
Neil Collins	Wood
Calvin Dixon	Central
Gordy Bryan	Malvern
Pat Purcell	Malvern
Roland Houston	King

1979
FIRST TEAM
Horace Owens	Dobbins
Kevin "Rock" McCray	W. Phila.
Ricky Tucker	Overbrook
Joe Washington	Overbrook
Lonnie McFarlan	Roman

SECOND TEAM
Steve Senko	Ryan
Kevin Beaford	Bok
Marty Campbell	Neumann
Mike McIntyre	Judge
Calvin Dixon	Central

THIRD TEAM
Carl Thomas	W. Cath.
Tom O'Hara	O'Hara
Joe Brown	Gratz
Terry "Doc" Watson	Dougherty
Vaughn Coats	Franklin
Rick Dennis	Lincoln

1980
FIRST TEAM

Lonnie McFarlan	Roman
Tony Costner	Overbrook
Marty Campbell	Neumann
Willie Oliphant	Northeast
Dallas Philson	Southern

SECOND TEAM

Bill Mitchell	O'Hara
Phil Burton	Franklin
Jerry Moore	W. Phila.
Ed Mostak	Ryan
James "Slurp" Gambrell	Edison

THIRD TEAM

Jerry "Jake" Sutton	Dougherty
Kevin "Cat" Compton	Frankford
Leon "Duke" Linder	Bartram
Mark Tarboro	Southern
Steve Black	Overbrook

1981
FIRST TEAM

Anthony Chennault	Frankford
Vic Alexander	Franklin
Jim Bolger	Kenrick
Terry Pittman	Gratz
Randy Monroe	Roman

SECOND TEAM

Ivan Felder	King
Keith Walker	Franklin
Glenn Welton	Roman
Steve Nesmith	Malvern
Charles Hickman	Episcopal

THIRD TEAM

John Bellinger	Edison
Chris O'Brien	La Salle
John Rousey	W. Cath.
John Luciano	Judge
Chip Greenberg	La Salle

1982
FIRST TEAM

Chip Greenberg	La Salle
Timmy Brown	Mastbaum
Rico Washington	Frankford
Gary Bennett	Central
Walt Fuller	Bonner

SECOND TEAM

Reggie Faison	Franklin
Darren Keith	Mastbaum
Dallas Comegys	Roman
Ronald Barnett	Olney
Anthony King	Penn

THIRD TEAM

Keith Coleman	SJ Prep
Mark Kelly	W. Cath.
Kenny Glass	Bartram
Timmy Pounds	Overbrook
Chris Blocker	Northeast

1983
FIRST TEAM

Dallas Comegys	Roman
Rico Washington	Franklin
Rodney Blake	Bonner
Mark Johnson	W. Cath.
James "Bruiser" Flint	Episcopal
Nate Blackwell	Southern

SECOND TEAM

Anthony Robinson	Edison
Rob Lawton	Roman
Brian Leahy	Kenrick
Jack Concannon	Bonner
Chris Blocker	Northeast

THIRD TEAM

Anthony McFadden	Olney
Howard Evans	W. Phila.
Tom Gormley	Bonner
Greg Jacobs	King
Ernest "Pop" Lewis	G-town

1984
FIRST TEAM

Rodney Blake	Bonner
Howard Evans	W. Phila.
Max Blank	Washing.
Michael Anderson	E&S
Jerome "Pooh" Richardson	Franklin

SECOND TEAM

Tarone Thornton	Roman
Brian Leahy	Kenrick
Troy Daniel	Lamber.
Henry Smith	W. Phila.
Greg "Bo" Kimble	Dobbins
Mark Stevenson	Roman

THIRD TEAM

Darin "Munchy" Mason	Mastbaum
Eric "Hank" Gathers	Dobbins
Steve Benton	Neumann
Brian "Sugar" Smith	Franklin
Craig Conlin	La Salle

1985
FIRST TEAM

Jerome "Pooh" Richardson	Franklin
Mark Stevenson	Roman
Greg "Bo" Kimble	Dobbins
Eric "Hank" Gathers	Dobbins
Steve Benton	Neumann

SECOND TEAM

Paul "Snoop" Graham	Franklin
Lionel Simmons	Southern
Craig Conlin	La Salle
Warren Hawthorne	Mastbaum
John Rankin	W. Cath.

THIRD TEAM

Barry Bekkedam	Carroll
Rick Williams	Gtn. Acad.
Otis Ellis	Gtn. Acad.
Brian Shorter	Gratz
Jonathan Jones	Central
Henry Jackson	Penn

1986
FIRST TEAM

Lionel Simmons	Southern
Brian Shorter	Gratz
Barry Bekkedam	Carroll
Ivan "Pick" Brown	Bonner
Dennis "Dink" Whitaker	Gratz

SECOND TEAM

Vincent "Butter" Smalls	U. City
Ernest Pollard	Roman
Ellis McKennie	Washing.
Marvin Walters	Gtn. Acad.
Reggie Isaac	Bartram
Rodney Jones	W. Phila.

THIRD TEAM

Ty "Magic" Cromwell	Mastbaum
Derreck Orr	Mastbaum
Kevin Cofield	Roman
Marshall Taylor	Southern
Mike Matthews	La Salle

1987
FIRST TEAM

Doug Overton	Dobbins
Robert "World" Stokes	Southern
Will Scott	Southern
Joe Jefferson	Edison
Mike Monroe	W. Phila.

SECOND TEAM

Vince Curran	SJ Prep
Eddie Savage	Gratz
Tom Dunn	Carroll
Clayton "Stink" Adams	Roman
Mike O'Hara	O'Hara

THIRD TEAM

James Glass	U. City
Larry Stewart	Dobbins
Ed McCrystal	Hav. Sch.
Jeff Hines	Episcopal
Harold Mobley	Washing.
Mike Kempski	Carroll

1988
FIRST TEAM
Brian Daly	Bonner
Mik Kilgore	W. Phila.
Randy Woods	Franklin
Monroe Blakes	W. Cath.
Brian Graves	Olney

SECOND TEAM
Gary Duda	Malvern
Carlin Warley	Frankford
Jim Schultice	N. Cath.
John O'Connell	McDevitt
Jamie Ross	Frankford

THIRD TEAM
Eric Williams	W. Phila.
Eddie Malloy	O'Hara
John Smedley	Ryan
Paul Chambers	Episcopal
Ed Jenkins	Roman
Craig White	Gtn. Acad.

1989
FIRST TEAM
Carlin Warley	Frankford
Alan Watkins	Roman
Chris Williams	Dougherty
Eddie Malloy	O'Hara
Mike Tyson	Overbrook

SECOND TEAM
Antoine Jefferson	Frank. L.C.
Phil "Sub" Crump	Franklin
Jason Warley	Frankford
Jonathan Haynes	Gtn. Fds.
Eugene Burroughs	Episcopal
Andre Daniel	Lamber.

THIRD TEAM
Aaron McKie	Gratz
Jim Rullo	Malvern
Corry Appline	Washing.
Kevin Benton	Mastbaum
Harry Moore	Gratz

1990
FIRST TEAM
Jonathan Haynes	Gtn. Fds.
Eugene Burroughs	Episcopal
Aaron McKie	Gratz
Kevin Benton	Mastbaum
Harry Moore	Gratz

SECOND TEAM
Kareem "Rab" Townes	Southern
Bernard Jones	Roman
Chris Mooney	Ryan
Roy Lloyd	W. Phila.
Kenya Mobley	Dobbins
Joe McEwing	Egan

THIRD TEAM
Tyrone Mason	Bartram
Faron "Meatball" Hand	Frank. L.C.
Damon Reid	Neumann
Chris Lazorcheck	La Salle
Jai Hill	Gir. Coll.

1991
FIRST TEAM
Kareem "Rab" Townes	Southern
Bernard Jones	Roman
Craig Wise	Central
Faron "Meatball" Hand	Frank. L.C.
Rasheed Wallace	Gratz
Tyrone Weeks	Frank. L.C.

SECOND TEAM
Paul Burke	C. Hill
Jerome Allen	Episcopal
Mike Watson	Roman
Marvin Harrison	Roman
Levan Alston	Gratz

THIRD TEAM
Marvin Stinson	Dobbins
Eric Moore	Episcopal
Shawn Newman	Dougherty
Tyrone Mason	Bartram
Phil "Weasel" Melton	Bartram

1992
FIRST TEAM

Rasheed Wallace	Gratz
Faron "Meatball" Hand	Frank. L.C.
Tyrone Weeks	Frank. L.C.
Jason Lawson	Olney
Cuttino "Cat" Mobley	Dougherty

SECOND TEAM

Adonal Foyle	O'Hara
Jeffery "Jay" Myers	Southern
Alvin Williams	Gtn. Acad.
Tim Krug	P. Charter
Malik Rose	Overbrook
Rondell Turner	U. City

THIRD TEAM

Amiri "Ralph" Johnson	Parkway
Wilbur Johnson	Central
Kyle Locke	Roman
Paul Favorite	Wood
Tyrone Tyson	Central

1993
FIRST TEAM

Rasheed Wallace	Gratz
Jason Lawson	Olney
Tyrone Weeks	Frank. L.C.
Alvin Williams	Gtn. Acad.
Marc Jackson	Roman

SECOND TEAM

Rondell Turner	Gratz
Laurence Pembrook	Overbrook
Ronald Kenan	Overbrook
Shawn "Reds" Smith	Gratz
Steve Goodrich	P. Charter
Mike Roberts	Carroll

THIRD TEAM

Devin Baker	W. Phila.
Antoine Brockington	Northeast
Anwar Amin	Bodine
Joe Harvey	N. Cath.
Mark Mulroy	Bonner

1994
FIRST TEAM

Lynard Stewart	Gratz
Rasiheed "Noot" Arnold	Frank. L.C.
Shawn "Reds" Smith	Gratz
Steve Goodrich	P. Charter
Michael Robinson	Frank. L.C.

SECOND TEAM

Rashid Bey	Neumann
Fred Warrick	Bok
Rasheed Brokenborough	U. City
Mike Gizzi	C. Hill
Alonzo Triplin	Olney

THIRD TEAM

Duane Johnson	Frankford
Lari Ketner	Roman
Brahin Riley	Northeast
Terrell Stokes	Gratz
Rafal Bigus	Carroll
Lormont Sharp	King

1995
FIRST TEAM

Rasheed Brokenborough	U. City
Terrell Stokes	Gratz
Lari Ketner	Roman
Rafal Bigus	Carroll
Andre Howard	Overbrook

SECOND TEAM

Joe Brown	Frank. L.C.
Donnie Carr	Roman
Dion Jones	Dobbins
Lynn Greer	E&S
Petrick Sanders	Frankford
Ryan Polley	Malvern

THIRD TEAM

Paul Romanczuk	Carroll
Mike Nestor	Bonner
Arthur "Yah" Davis	Roman
Ben Davis	Malvern
Jermaine Ballow	Southern

1996
FIRST TEAM
Donnie Carr	Roman
Arthur "Yah" Davis	Frankford
Malik Moore	King
Petrick Sanders	Frankford
Abdul Taylor	Audenried

SECOND TEAM
Omar Logan	Edison
Marvin O'Connor	Gratz
Lynn Greer	E&S
Eric Coleman	Frank. L.C.
Martin Ingelsby	Carroll
Julius Williams	Gtn. Acad.

THIRD TEAM
Anwar "Fis" Blackmon	U. City
Albert Crockett	Edison
N'aim Crenshaw	Overbook
Ronnie Conway	Frankford
Dy Cameron	Hav. Sch.

1997
FIRST TEAM
Lynn Greer	E&S
Marvin O'Connor	Gratz
Jarett Kearse	Gratz
Martin Ingelsby	Carroll
N'aim Crenshaw	Overbrook
Victor Thomas	Neumann

SECOND TEAM
Julius Williams	Gtn. Acad.
John Phillips	Episcopal
Kevin "Buzzy" Forney	Mansion
Chris Krug	Gtn. Acad.
Bill Phillips	Carroll

THIRD TEAM
James Fowler	Neumann
Sharif Brown	Bok
Rasual Butler	Roman
Anwar Scott	C. Grove
John Ashmore	W. Cath.

1998
FIRST TEAM
Rasual Butler	Roman
Alex Wesby	Franklin
Chris Krug	Gtn. Acad.
Kevin "Buzzy" Forney	Mansion
Jim Reeves	Judge

SECOND TEAM
Devon Fowler	Neumann
Tom Whitworth	C. Hill
Brian Burke	Gtn. Acad.
Zakee Smith	Frank. L.C.
John Phillips	Episcopal
Will Chavis	E&S

THIRD TEAM
Alex Sazonov	O'Hara
Adam Brown	Penn
Anthony Starace	Ryan
Rahim Washington	Overbrook
John Ashmore	W. Cath.

1999
FIRST TEAM
Eddie Griffin	Roman
John Cox	E&S
Calvin Johnson	Franklin
Doug Fairfax	Hav. Sch.
Randy Dukes	Northeast
Jermaine Robinson	Gratz

SECOND TEAM
Kasim Holloman	SJ Prep
Tim Whitworth	C. Hill
Ashley Howard	Bonner
Jeff Randazzo	O'Hara
Kareem Pilgrim	Lamberton

THIRD TEAM
Sean Knitter	P. Charter
Mike Pidhirsky	Judge
Gerald Redding	Frankford
Jason Dunham	Franklin
Tim Whalen	Wood

CATHOLIC LEAGUE

HIGHEST SEASON AVERAGE BY SCHOOL

School	Name	G-Pts.	Avg.	Year
Bonner	Ashley Howard	14-333	23.8	1999
Carroll	Barry Bekkedam	14-330	23.6	1986
Conwell-Egan	Brian Townsend	16-296	18.5	1974
Dougherty	Terry "Doc" Watson	16-364	22.8	1979
Judge	George Sutor	15-304	20.3	1961
Kenn.-Kenrick	Jeff Kane	14-247	17.6	1999
Kenrick	Jim Bolger	16-353	22.1	1981
La Salle	Tom Gola	13-335	25.8	1951
McDevitt	Dan Kelly	12-276	23.0	1966
Neumann	Steve Benton	14-295	21.1	1985
North	Hank Siemiontkowski	16-361	22.6	1968
	Joe Schoen	16-361	22.6	1977
O'Hara	Fran Grandieri	14-325	23.2	2000
Roman	Donnie Carr	14-380	27.1	1996
Ryan	Anthony Starace	14-344	24.6	1998
St. James	Bill Lynch	14-352	25.1	1952
SJ Prep	Kasim Holloman	14-341	24.4	1999
ST More	Mike Jones	16-419	26.2	1969
West	Monroe Blakes	14-385	27.5	1988
Wood	Tim Whalen	14-287	20.5	1999

Record: 27.5, Monroe Blakes, West Catholic, 14-385, 1988.

INTER-AC

HIGHEST SEASON AVERAGE BY SCHOOL

School	Name	G-Pts.	Avg.	Year
Chestnut Hill	Tom Whitworth	10-263	26.3	1998
Episcopal	James "Bruiser" Flint	10-221	22.1	1983
Gtn. Academy	Paul Hutter	9-236	26.2	1970
Haver. School	Doug Fairfax	10-283	28.3	1999
Malvern	Pat Purcell	10-260	26.0	1978
Penn Charter	Billy Harris	9-258	28.7	1971

Record: 28.7, Billy Harris, Penn Charter, 9-258, 1971.

PUBLIC LEAGUE

HIGHEST SEASON AVERAGE BY SCHOOL

School	Name	G-Pts.	Avg.	Year
Audenried	Abdul Taylor	15-444	29.6	1996
Bartram	Reggie Isaac	13-405	31.2	1986
Bodine	Eric White	10-381	38.1	1991
Bok	Kevin Beaford	15-415	27.7	1979
Central	Craig Wise	10-333	33.3	1991
Dobbins	Horace Owens	15-439	29.3	1979
Edison	Melvin Eason	13-384	29.5	1998
Eng. & Science	Michael Anderson	12-375	31.3	1984
Fels	Nile Patrick	7-148	21.1	2000
Frankford	John Scott	10-250	25.0	1955
Franklin	Ira Miles	14-398	28.4	1967
Franklin L.C.	Joe Brown	10-306	30.6	1995
Furness	Jamal Lomax	8-251	31.4	1993
GAMP	Kyle Locke	14-302	21.6	1990
Germantown	Calvin Gore	12-325	27.1	1956
Gratz	Brian Shorter	13-416	32.0	1986
Kensington	David Rivera	10-214	21.4	1998
King	Dawan Robinson	13-410	31.5	2000
Lamberton	Troy Daniel	12-385	32.1	1984
Lincoln	Larry Cannon	14-492	35.1	1965
Mastbaum	Kevin Benton	12-333	27.8	1990
Masterman	Shawn Munford	15-341	22.7	1996
Northeast (n)	Randy Dukes	13-412	31.7	1999
Northeast (o)	Guy Rodgers	12-417	34.8	1953
Olney	Willie Taylor	14-396	28.3	1972
Overbrook	Wilt Chamberlain	12-566	47.2	1955
Parkway	Amiri "Ralph" Johnson	8-196	24.5	1991
Penn	Jerome Brisbon	13-369	28.4	1982
Phila. Reg.	Mike Latham	6-116	19.3	1994
Roxborough	Walter "Buddy" Harris	14-474	33.9	1966
Southern	Kareem "Rab" Townes	9-371	41.2	1991
Straw. Mans.	Omar Thomas	13-306	23.5	2000
Univ. City	Rash. Brokenborough	11-284	25.8	1993
Washington	Ellis McKennie	13-412	31.7	1986
West	Ray "Chink" Scott	12-380	31.7	1956

Record: 47.2, Wilt Chamberlain, Overbrook, 12-566, 1955.

LEAGUE CHAMPIONS

PUBLIC LEAGUE

1911	Central	1914 Southern	1917 Southern
1912	Northeast	1915 Northeast	1918 Northeast
1913	Central	1916 Central	1919 West Phila.

	PUBLIC	CATHOLIC	INTER-AC
1920	Southern	St. Joseph's Prep	—
1921	West Phila.	West Catholic	—
1922	Southern	Roman Catholic	—
1923	West Phila.	St. Joseph's Prep	—
1924	West Phila.	Roman Catholic	Haverford School
1925	Southern	Roman Catholic	Haverford School
1926	Southern	Roman Catholic	Penn Charter
1927	Northeast	Roman Catholic	Haverford School
1928	West Phila.	Roman Catholic	Haverford School
1929	Northeast	North Catholic	Episcopal
1930	Southern	Roman Catholic	Gtn. Academy
1931	Overbrook	West Catholic	Friends' Central
1932	Central	North Catholic	*Penn Charter
			*Chestnut Hill
1933	Southern	Roman Catholic	*Chestnut Hill
			*Episcopal
1934	*Gratz	Roman Catholic	Penn Charter
	*Overbrook		
	*West Phila.		
1935	Overbrook	North Catholic	*Haverford School
			*Penn Charter
1936	Southern	La Salle	Penn Charter
1937	Southern	La Salle	Haverford School
1938	Southern	West Catholic	Penn Charter
1939	Gratz	South Catholic	Friends' Central
1940	Southern	South Catholic	Penn Charter
1941	West Phila.	South Catholic	Penn Charter
1942	West Phila.	La Salle	Penn Charter
1943	West Phila.	Roman	Penn Charter
1944	Bartram	South Catholic	Penn Charter
1945	Southern	South Catholic	*Friends' Central
			*Penn Charter
1946	Southern	La Salle	Friends' Central
1947	Bartram	St. Joseph's Prep	Friends' Central
1948	Overbrook	La Salle	Penn Charter

1949	Overbrook	West Catholic	Haverford School
1950	Overbrook	La Salle	Haverford School
1951	West Phila.	St. Thomas More	*Haverford School *Penn Charter
1952	Franklin	West Catholic	Penn Charter
1953	Overbrook	West Catholic	Penn Charter
1954	Overbrook	South Catholic	Gtn. Academy
1955	Overbrook	West Catholic	Penn Charter
1956	West Phila.	North Catholic	Penn Charter
1957	Overbrook	North Catholic	Haverford School
1958	Overbrook	Neumann	*Haverford School *Malvern Prep
1959	Overbrook	West Catholic	*Gtn. Academy *Malvern Prep
1960	West Phila.	Bonner	Malvern Prep
1961	Bartram	St. Thomas More	*Malvern Prep *Penn Charter
1962	West Phila.	St. Joseph's Prep	Penn Charter
1963	West Phila.	La Salle	Penn Charter
1964	Germantown	Dougherty	Penn Charter
1965	Lincoln	Neumann	Malvern Prep
1966	Edison	St. Thomas More	Malvern Prep
1967	Overbrook	North Catholic	Gtn. Academy
1968	West Phila.	O'Hara	Gtn. Academy
1969	Edison	Roman Catholic	*Gtn. Academy *Haverford School *Penn Charter
1970	Overbrook	Dougherty	Penn Charter
1971	Overbrook	St. Joseph's Prep	*Episcopal *Penn Charter
1972	Bartram	St. Thomas More	Penn Charter
1973	Gratz	Roman Catholic	Malvern Prep
1974	West Phila.	Roman Catholic	Malvern Prep
1975	West Phila.	Father Judge	*Haverford School *Malvern Prep
1976	West Phila.	Kenrick	Malvern Prep
1977	West Phila.	Judge	Malvern Prep
1978	West Phila.	Roman Catholic	Haverford School
1979	Overbrook	Roman Catholic	Episcopal
1980	Overbrook	Roman Catholic	Episcopal
1981	Franklin	La Salle	Malvern Prep

1982	Mastbaum	Roman Catholic	Episcopal
1983	Overbrook	Bonner	Episcopal
1984	Franklin	Bonner	Penn Charter
1985	Dobbins	Neumann	Gtn. Academy
1986	Southern	Roman Catholic	Penn Charter
1987	Southern	North Catholic	Episcopal
1988	Frankford	Bonner	*Episcopal
			*Penn Charter
1989	Frankford	Roman Catholic	Episcopal
1990	Gratz	Roman Catholic	Episcopal
1991	Gratz	Roman Catholic	Episcopal
1992	Franklin L.C.	Roman Catholic	*Chestnut Hill
			*Gtn. Academy
1993	Gratz	Roman Catholic	Gtn. Academy
1994	Gratz	Roman Catholic	*Chestnut Hill
			*Penn Charter
1995	Univ. City	Carroll	*Gtn. Academy
			*Malvern Prep
1996	Edison	Roman Catholic	Gtn. Academy
1997	Gratz	Neumann	Gtn. Academy
1998	Franklin	Judge	*Chestnut Hill
			*Gtn. Academy
1999	Franklin	Roman Catholic	Haverford School
2000	S. Mansion	Roman Catholic	Gtn. Academy

* Tied for League Title

Champions determined by regular-season record except Public League (1919, '30, '32-35, '39-99) and Catholic League (1923, '25, '37, '42-99).

CITY CHAMPIONS

Year	City Titlist
1939	Gratz
1940	Southern
1941	South Catholic
1942	West Philadelphia
1943	West Philadelphia
1944	Bartram
1945	South Catholic
1946	La Salle
1947	St. Joseph's Prep
1948	La Salle
1949	West Catholic
1950	La Salle
1951	St. Thomas More
1952	West Catholic
1953	West Catholic
1954	Overbrook
1955	Overbrook
1956	North Catholic
1957	Overbrook
1958	Overbrook
1959	Overbrook
1960	Monsignor Bonner
1961	St. Thomas More
1962	West Philadelphia
1963	West Philadelphia
1964	Germantown
1965	Bishop Neumann
1966	Edison
1967	North Catholic
1968	West Philadelphia
1969	Edison
1970	Overbrook
1971	Overbrook
1972	St. Thomas More
1973	No game
1974	Roman Catholic
1975	West Philadelphia
1976	West Philadelphia
1977	West Philadelphia
1978	West Philadelphia
1979	Overbrook
1980	Overbrook

Staff of the *Philadelphia Daily News*

EDITORS: Paul Vigna, Jeff Samuels

DESIGN: Jon Snyder

EXECUTIVE SPORTS EDITOR: Pat McLoone

SPORTS EDITOR: Caesar Alsop

CONTRIBUTORS: Ed Barkowitz, Bill Conlin, Bob Cooney, Sam Donnellon, Bernard Fernandez, Bill Fleischman, Rich Hofmann, Phil Jasner, Dick Jerardi, Mike Kern, Mark Kram, Tom Mahon, Cecil Mosenson, Kevin Mulligan, Dana Pennett O'Neil, Leigh Primavera, Ted Silary, John Smallwood, Bob Vetrone Jr.

COPY EDITORS: Josh Barnett, Chuck Bausman, Joe Berkery, Doug Darroch, Jim DeStefano, Drew McQuade, Debbie Woodell

SPECIAL THANKS: Carla Shultzberg, University of Pennsylvania; Carola Cifaldi, Immaculata College; Sonny Hill; Littel Vaughn

---

Chapter Opener Photo Credits